Healed,
In Jesus' Name

SAM O. ADEWUNMI

COVENANT PUBLISHING

Healed, In Jesus' Name
Sam O. Adewunmi

Unless otherwise stated, all scripture quotations are taken from the Holy Bible, New King James Version (NKJV). Other versions cited are NIV, KJV, GNB, God's Word, MSG, LEB and NLT.

ISBN 978-1-907734-06-9
First Edition, First Printing November 2015

No part of this publication may be produced, distorted or transmitted in any form or by any means, including photocopying, recording or other electronic or mechanical methods, without the prior written permission of the publisher, or except in the case of brief quotations embodied in critical reviews and certain other non-commercial uses permitted by copyright law.

For permission requests, write to the publisher, addressed "Attention: Permission Coordinator" at the email address:

Covenant Publishing
samadewunmi@btinternet.com
Covenant Publishing is part of New Covenant Church
Charity Registered in England & Wales number 1004343
Registered Address: 506-510 Old Kent Road. LONDON SE1 5BA

Copyright © November 2015, Sam O. Adewunmi

Cover Design by Covenant Publishing Team
Sam Adewunmi's photo by David Adetoye
Published by Covenant Publishing
Printed in the United Kingdom

ENDORSEMENTS

Healed, in Jesus' Name, is a scripturally and scientifically sound book reinforced by Pastor Sam's personal experience of healing. The case for healing in this book is captivating and compelling, and the balanced place allotted to modern medicine is highly insightful.

> Dr. T. Ayodele Ajayi, MRCPsych
> Author, Footprints of Giants
> General Adult Psychiatrist
> Director Mentor into Medicine

My ardent wish had been to find someone who will be able to give an unbiased clarity to the role of medicine and the belief in God as our healer. In *Healed, in Jesus' Name*, Reverend Sam has been able to tease out and unravel my wish. He articulated and tried to bridge the gap between medicine and faith which has been a challenge especially for those of us who believe in Christ and also practice medicine.

The first surgical and anesthetic procedure was performed on Adam during the time Eve was created. Since that time, God gave us the knowledge to treat i.e. ameliorate and remove symptoms, but only He can heal i.e. restore to full health and vitality. This is what Reverend Adewunmi is testifying to in this book.

The in-depth research done and the scriptural back-up indicate to me that God's word is forever sure and does not need updating. Our knowledge will forever need to be updated as the Lord opens our mind to more innovations and ideas.

The devil has no other weapon but ignorance and deception. It is, however, unfortunate that a lot of Christians have died, suffered and are still dying and suffering in ill health for lack of knowledge about the role of medicine and faith. That is why the bible says my people perish for lack of knowledge (Hosea 4:6). The scripture also says, "Howbeit when the Spirit of Truth shall come, He would guide us into all truth" (John 16:13), and the Truth "is the Word Himself that dwelt amongst us" (John 1:14).

As a Medical Doctor, and a Christian, I believe that no medical knowledge or ability can stop the work of God or contest with His power. He is God all by Himself, and there is no other. I pray that as you read *Healed, in Jesus' Name,* the Lord would open your heart to the new dimension of His power that work inwards and outwards and will bring healing to your whole being in Jesus' name.

Healed, in Jesus' Name is a very inspiring book and I am extremely privileged to recommend this book for reading and healing.

Dr. Olaniyi Ajayi, MBChB, MsC, DipOccmed
Deputy Clinical and Dual Diagnosis Lead
Turning Point: East Kent Substance Misuse Service,
United Kingdom

I very strongly recommend this book to anyone struggling with any medical condition in order that you can identify with this great testimony to strengthen your faith and lay hold of the vast number of Scriptures within the book (relating to specific medical disorders) to receive your healing.

There are many things (symptoms or disorders) in medicine that remains unexplained despite the vast improvement and advancement in diagnostic equipment and procedures but God Almighty, Jesus Christ, can explain all. God is the source of all truth and wisdom and the answer to any doubts that, this degree of burns can completely heal so fast can only be found in Jesus Christ alone and to whomever He chooses to reveal it.

I believe in the miracle of healing because I have also personally experienced it and even as a Medical Doctor knew that it was not medically plausible, only Jesus Christ could do such miracles. To Jesus Christ alone be all the glory for this wonderful testimony.

Dr. Darlington Daniel
Consultant General Adult & Liaison Psychiatrist
Associate Medical Director
(Havering Integrated Care Directorate, NELFT, UK)

TABLE OF CONTENTS

Endorsements
Dedication
Acknowledgement
Foreword

Chapters
Introduction - Say 'Yes' to Healing   15
1 - Healed of Burns   19
2 - 'Jesus', the Most Powerful Name   29
3 - Healing is God's Will   35
4 - Diseases Have Spirits   49
5 - Sicknesses Are Transferred at Night 57
6 - Causes of Sicknesses   65
7 - Documented Healing in the New
    Testament   83
8 - Healed, In Jesus' Name   87
9 - Healing Scriptures   95
10 - "This Belongs to Me"   137
11 - It Makes Sense   143

DEDICATION

This book is dedicated to the memory of my late junior brother who passed into eternity on April 23, 2011 of a heart attack whilst playing football in the country of Nigeria. Adebayo Olanrewaju Adewunmi, you are sorely missed. We love you but God loves you more.

ACKNOWLEDGEMENT

To the immortal God Who spared my life to be able to pen this book - Lord, I 'shachah' (shaw-khaw, bow down) before You. No life can exist without You Lord. You are the giver and keeper of life. I now understand Your wisdom.

To my sweetheart and friend, my wife of over 23 years, I really appreciate you for taking good care of me during my ordeal and recovery. Toyin, Ademi (My Crown), you did what nobody else on earth could do to make me comfortable. You took time off work just for me, and checked on me every time when you were back at work. Thank you dear. Love you to the moon and back.

My wonderful children, Ayomikun, Fikayomi, and Mayokun, thank you for bearing with me and running all the errands.

To my church family, you are the best. Your prayers and support meant a lot to me and I will forever be grateful to you for standing by me.

A special thank you goes to Elder Peter Agbontaen and Sister Augusta Oke. Elder Peter took over the running of the business without being asked to until I was fit enough to return.

Sister Augusta visited while I was still very sore at home.

To all the ER Staff at Queen Elizabeth Hospital, Woolwich, London and the Team at the specialist burnt unit at Chelsea and Westminster Hospital also in London, your care made the difference and only heaven can pay you back. I really appreciate you.

FOREWORD

I was touched by the very first chapter of this book as it brought to my remembrance a young man in my church who had a similar burn experience when he accidentally poured oil on his right leg. He could not handle the pain and he cursed Jesus. He could not handle why God would allow such a thing to happen to him. He was transferred to the Burns Unit of a hospital in South West London. He had assured God he would not go to church anymore. His leg was not healing and visitors could not visit him because of the pungent smell on the ward. He was informed on a Tuesday of an impending amputation the next day because the poison in his leg was spreading and would eventually kill him.

He asked God for forgiveness and retracted all he had said against the Almighty. A couple of hours later the ward lit up and he heard a voice, "You came to this country with two legs and would return with two legs." On Wednesday morning, two nurses turned up to undo his bandages and to prepare him for the amputation. Both screamed upon looking at his legs. The gangrene had disappeared and a fresh flesh had appeared. The Chinese consultant could not believe his eyes. He had never believed in God and this to him was impossible to accept. He finally resigned as a medical doctor to return home in Shanghai, China. He has now become a pastor in an underground church in the region of Shanghai serving Jesus.

Sam kept calling the name of Jesus because he knew he owned the name of Jesus. He has accepted the word of God as truth and that was what he proclaimed. After eleven days, his face had no traces of burning to date. What a miracle! Sam has enumerated some healing scriptures for your reading and acceptance; healing will definitely follow. He has a measure of research into some killer diseases and assurance of the promises of God to combat all those fears. I am no stranger to healings and miracles.

I strongly recommend this book to you. I see healings virtually every day because I initiate it and Jesus manifests it.

Revd. Major Sam Larbie (Rtd)

Pastor, Elim Pentecostal Church, Rushey Green
Author, Healing is Easy

INTRODUCTION

Say 'Yes' to Healing

Do you know the power in the name of Jesus in healing? Are you aware of the sources of sickness and diseases? What does the Bible have to say about healing and God's will? Are spirits involved in sicknesses? How are diseases and sicknesses transferred? Where are the healing scriptures in the Bible? What is the role of Medicine in biblical healing?

These and many more questions are answered in this inspiring book.

First, I have this to say.

Several years ago, I undertook to write a book on healing. I collected materials from shelves

HEALED, IN JESUS' NAME

everywhere and as many bookstores as I could find. My motive was to discover if healing is for our generation and to prove our brothers (who claim that healing ceased) right or wrong. At the time, I had laid hands on a few people to receive healing, and they were all healed. However, I was told it was psychological and not spiritual. So I began to search the scriptures for truth. And truth, I found. The more I studied, the more I became convinced that healing is still for our generation, and all generations and that healing is a believer's right. I became concerned that the devil had cheated us from enjoying this God-given blessing for a long time.

Some of the books I read are: Healing Scriptures by Kenneth E Hagin; Healing Scriptures by Joyce Meyers; Healing Scriptures by Sid Roth (e-book); Smith Wigglesworth on Healing by Smith Wigglesworth; Healed of Cancer by Dodie Osteen; Divine Healing by Andrew Murray; God's Medicine Bottle by Derek Prince; Healing Belongs to Us by Kenneth E Hagin; How to Keep your Healing by Kenneth E Hagin; Inspirations from the Miracles of Jesus by Andrew Lloyd Adeleke; Healing is Easy by Sam Larbie; and Healing Promises by Kenneth and Gloria Copeland.

Introduction - Say 'Yes' To Healing

The books gave several approaches to healing. Each touched on different aspects of the subject. But I felt there was more. So I set out to add my insight on the subject and experiences on the healing line to those of these generals.

For some unexplainable reasons, the urge, determination and inspiration to write became elusive and began to dwindle with time. This made me consign writing on the subject to the future and the realm of 'maybe-God-does-not-want-me-to-write-on-healing' thinking. I, therefore, delved into the arena of writing on purposeful living, financial independence, character building, spirituality and morality. This gave me my first shot at writing four published titles.

Years later, I had a terrible accident - one that made an indelible mark on me. I had a fire accident and my face was totally burnt. All I had was the name of Jesus. Whilst burning, and without thinking, I shouted 'Jesus' out loud. That name started my healing process.

This book details the fire accident that happened to me and the healing power of God that got me back on my feet from a second-degree burn within eleven days. I do not consider my healing or myself special. God can heal you if you want. This is not a book just on healing burns. It is a book on healing arthritis, cancer, barrenness, tumours, raised blood pressure, kidney and liver problems, heart disease, depression, migraine, anaemia, leukaemia, diabetes, asthma and many more.

Do you want to be 'Healed, in Jesus' Name'? Say 'Yes' and start reading.

CHAPTER 1

Healed of Burns

It was an ordinary day, or so it seemed. The sun shone brightly in the sky, and the temperature was above normal for this time of the year. September 18th, 2014 will forever be a memorable day, at least for me. Come to think of it, that was exactly a week after the annual remembrance of the September 11. Umm, would it matter? No, I do not know, but it was just a thought.

I took the day off work so I could prepare something nice for my growing church family. In three days, it was going to be my birthday. It was not a special birthday except that it was going to fall on a Sunday. "Why not treat our church to a barbecue meal?" I thought to myself. I know what you are thinking right now. Yes, you are right. I could have contracted it out. What does pastoring have in common with cooking? I might answer that later.

But I thought to myself, "Why should I have to pay someone to do it?" My wife is an excellent cook, and I am superb at barbecuing. I derive some pleasure in doing it. I've been doing this for the last 20 years. In fact, I barbecued until November of 2013. Our grill only gets to go into the shed for just five months of the year. That is how much I love barbecue and making it. So I took the day off.

I got out the grill set and lit the charcoal. Everything was going on well until the second batch, and there were only going to be three batches. I set the cooking heat to medium as I wanted the meat to be well done. As a result, I lost most of the heat and the kindle. I then set aside the cooked meat (the first batch) and began to fan the dying coal. Nothing happened. I then decided to add some combustible liquid. Again, nothing seemed to happen.

As if I was watching a movie, as I got closer to take a look, the set exploded right in my face.

Chapter 1 - Healed of Burns

Just like that, I was ablaze. I lost any sense of my surrounding. "Where am I? Am I alive or am I dead? In hell or earth, where am I?" Those were the questions that ran through my mind. Though it was only a second, it felt like I just opened a door to a house on fire. I was thrown from one end of the garden to the other. In the process, my pair of slippers snapped with each ending up at different spots in the backyard. The fuel bottle slipped as I staggered away from the grill set, and I was fortunate it did not drain on me. Otherwise, it would have been a worse scenario.

Inside the fire was a figure that looked like an 'angel of death'. I saw it; it was so real. The devil had come for me, but God was with me. I remember shouting the name 'Jesus.' I continued shouting the name as I started running for help. The children were at school; my wife was at work, and I was alone by myself. I quickly picked myself up as a soldier ready to fight, ran into the house and started pacing the floor. I still cannot tell where and how I got the energy.

What am I to do now, call my wife or the emergency services? I quickly reached out for the phone and could not be bothered whether it was a mobile or land line. I desperately needed help. I was burning. In a split second, the person I thought fit to call was my wife. She would give me the best care. She would attend to me like no other. After all, she is my wife. She knows my frame and my need. Above all, she'd been in the nursing profession for over 30 years and currently working as an Occupational Health and Well-being Manager with a reputable London University. I called her, so sure I had made the right decision.

I called her mobile phone and the office land line, both kept ringing, but no one answered. I knew I had the right numbers as I had used them over the years. I know them by heart. Oh yes! I had my wife's voice, but it was only the pre-recorded message. That was not what I needed, so I went to plan B and dialled 999. It would be another four hours before I would find out she went to a meeting in another office and had left her mobile phone behind. The devil had everything well planned, but God gave me a little strength. Remember, I was all alone in the house, but for God, I would have died before anyone arrived home.

By this time, I had lost much water and protein fluid from the burns. It stung so harshly, and I was in excruciating pain. I was asked by the control room operator to describe the pain I was having to any other I had ever experienced. All I could say to him was that there was

Chapter 1 - Healed of Burns

nothing comparable. Friends, I am not kidding - I had not experienced anything worse in my life. The fire was long dead, but the burning had just only begun. The emergency personnel then told me that help was on the way and that I should run water over the affected areas for at least 10 minutes. That meant I had to strip completely as my chest, and my right arm were also affected.

I could not stay under running water for ten minutes as I was desperately awaiting the arrival of the medics. Joyfully, every minute spent under the tap brought relief, suppressed the sting and was soothing. I wished I could have carried on under the tap for longer. However, I got quickly dressed and before I could put my top back on; I had the sound of the doorbell.

Finally!! Help arrived. First it was the car ambulance. Waiting for a van ambulance could have taken longer perhaps, they thought. After ensuring I was very alert and conscious, the medic that attended to me excused himself in order to make a quick call. Apparently, "the whole of London is on the way to my house," he said, meaning that, all the emergency services were rushing to my rescue. Well, his call was too late. Within two minutes, my street was littered with ambulances, fire engines, and more paramedics in vans. This is to show the perceived severity of my accident. After narrating the incident to the medics, for more than ten times as I could vividly count and recollect, they kept saying I was "very lucky". Their expectation was worse, going by their experience. Glory be to God.

After assessing my condition and concluding that there was no possibility of the fire rekindling, all the emergency services except the van ambulance left. I was then taken to Queen Elizabeth Hospital where I was further examined, treated, and the degree of the burn established. The hospital was unexpectedly busy on the day such that I was treated by a junior doctor several hours later. After several results had come in, it was decided I had to be referred to a Specialist Burns Unit at Chelsea and Westminster Hospital, being the closest Burns Unit to where I live. I could not travel on the public transport with the burnt face. Even when I drove to the hospital for treatment, heads would turn in disgust and bemusement. I became a scorn.

I had read several stories of fire casualties - the scars, the deformities, the skin tones; nothing was going to be as before. I was informed it would take years before anyone would be able to recognise me as I was before the burn. Then, I

Chapter 1 - Healed of Burns

began to pray that I would have a different experience. I had prayed for people who needed God's touch in the area of healing, but it never crossed my mind that I would need Him to heal me next. He did, and it was so speedy.

By the fourth day, the scabs started lifting, and it was so quick that I was forced to take my first selfie by the sixth day. I said to myself, "No one would believe my story unless there was a proof." Within eleven days, the scabs on my chest, arm and face were all gone. All that was left was the little redness on my face and my lips. The nurses and doctors were so impressed by the speed of recovery that I got discharged from the hospital the third visit, which was the eleventh day. They concluded I "healed quickly." Well, Jesus healed me quickly.

Three times before the accident, God revealed there was an impending accident but did not disclose the specifics. When at first I had a revelation, I prayed about it and considered it settled. When I had a second encounter, I had to tell the church, and we prayed fervently on the day. In my mind, the synergy settled it. However, before I could inform anybody of the third encounter, the devil struck. The incident happened on one of our bible study days, and I was to teach on the day. Upon hearing the news

HEALED, IN JESUS' NAME

of the accident, the church went into another praying mode. I believe the revelations and the prayers of the saint saved me. My 2014 birthday would have been my burial, and I would not have seen 2015.

If you are a true worshiper and are busy for God; that upsets the devil. I am not praising myself; this is just the truth. At the time of the incident, our Church was in the second week of our Praise Month. Every Sunday in September, year in year out, we do no other activity but praise God. Maybe you did not know; I love worship, and I can lead worship. So I led worship the first Sunday. The third Sunday was my birthday and Pastor Emmanuel King, our guest minister, a highly anointed man of God, was to lead worship on the day. Can you now imagine why the devil was upset?

To make matters worse, the incident happened three weeks to our European Ministers Convention. The devil did everything possible to take me out, but God prevailed. For 2014, I chaired the National Events Committee of the New Covenant Church UK, and the Convention was our biggest event. We had been planning and praying for a spectacular supernatural visitation at the convention, and God made it possible for me to witness it,

Chapter 1 - Healed of Burns

despite my ordeal. I was to be the convener at the convention. By this time, all the redness on my face had disappeared to the point that just about three people wondered why my lips were reddish.

Two things God did to save me. I had initially set up the grill set by the back door leading to our kitchen so I could reduce my movements to just an arm's length since there were no other helping hands. If the accident occurred at the entrance to the kitchen, our new kitchen and perhaps the whole house could have been raised to the ground. Also, I could have fallen into several sharp objects cluttered around the back door entrance and would have bled to death. However, for some reason, I decided to move the set exactly to the middle of the garden just before the accident.

The second is this - I had my highly flammable top, made of Nylon, taken off. For some reason, I felt sweltering and was uncomfortable right in the middle of September. So I had to take my top off leaving me with just a vest (singlet). If I had not, the top could have caught the fire and no doubt, I could have burnt to death with just me at the house. Thank you, Jesus.

HEALED, IN JESUS' NAME

I did not miss my birthday, the praise month and the convention. In fact, we had the barbecue on my birthday as planned. To God be the glory, and honour, for evermore. Amen.

There are some questions and concerns that were raised by those who read my story on the internet and the social media. My responses are given at the end of this book.

CHAPTER 2

'Jesus', The Most Powerful Name

Demons tremble at the name of Jesus. The name 'Jesus', is more potent than any missile or weapon of warfare. You could well be in Cuenca, Ecuador and use the name of Jesus to command change in Subang Jaya, Malaysia, a distance of 12,421 miles apart, and it will happen. No other name carries as much power and influence as the name of Jesus.

I remember the birth of our last son. The pregnant mum was to go to work when she woke up from a dream. In the dream, she saw an accident was to happen at the office building work. So we concluded that she should take a day off and rest. She was only weeks from

HEALED, IN JESUS' NAME

delivery of the baby but was still working to keep active. At home, she decided to tidy and clean the house in other to maintain being active.

Then at night, she started bleeding, and we immediately drove to the accident and emergency unit of the hospital closest to us. Investigations were conducted, and two abnormalities were discovered. We agreed together in prayer that night, and I was sent home to sleep. I was home by myself because our other children had been taken in by a friend. Rarely did I know I was in for a spiritual battle.

I had this dream. In the dream, I was inside a building that had two entrances, and I was talking to a Christian brother. Then I saw a deceased Church sister approaching the building. I immediately said to myself, "What is the dead doing among the living?" She walked in my direction as she approached the entrance to the building. I knew it was not right. So I began to shout 'Jesus, Jesus' on the top of my voice.

The lady became uncomfortable and ran towards the brother who was standing by me. I continued to shout the name, and she became even more nervous and could not touch the brother also. When I realised it worked, I shouted the more. She then exited through the

Chapter 2 - 'Jesus', The Most Powerful Name

other door, and I followed after her shouting still 'Jesus.' We both got out of the building, and I saw her suddenly rushing towards my pregnant wife who was out in the open getting some fresh air. I had more reasons to shout louder. And, I did. The lady became even more agitated and could not touch my wife either because I called 'Jesus.' Still, I followed after her, and she turned into a whirlwind and disappeared in the whirlwind. Glory to God.

I was still shouting 'Jesus, Jesus, Jesus' when I woke up. Had anyone been at home with me, I would have embarrassed them or be perceived as someone who had just lost it. I carried on calling the name until I was now exhausted and I drifted off back to sleep. I received the interpretation to the dream in a vision the same morning. The angel of death, impersonating the deceased sister, was on a mission to kill both my wife and the pregnancy. However, the name 'Jesus' did it for us.

I arrived the hospital to the news that the two issues we prayed about the night before had been resolved. However, further investigations revealed a rare condition that would have meant that the boy would have died, had my wife gone into labour from home. Speaking to her later, she also told me of the dream she had the same night. I would withhold the details of her dream for another time.

Not knowing the power in the name of Jesus is the greatest loss to power availed a child of God. Not having the right to use the name is the saddest tragedy that would ever befall a person. Every miracle performed in the entire New Testament was in the power of the Holy Spirit, through the shed blood of Christ, and in the name of Jesus. There was no single miracle without the name of Jesus being used.

Jesus is the physician

There was a dear brother who visited the hospital from work complaining of severe stomach pain. He was admitted to the hospital, and investigations were carried out. None of the investigations proved conclusive. They ran another series of tests but were unable to diagnose anything treatable. His case made the physicians look untaught. Yet, they ran the tests again but concluded it was beyond reasoning. So they asked if he had a minister to come and visit him just in case they might lose him.

The call came into the office when all the senior ministers had gone home. I was the only

Chapter 2 - 'Jesus', The Most Powerful Name

one left in the building completing a task that I was assigned. I took up the challenge, rose to the occasion, went to the hospital, laid my hands on him and, in the name of Jesus, commanded him to be released. Minutes later, the light of God shone on the problem, and he was rightfully diagnosed and treated. 20 years on, he is still alive.

Prayer of innocence, in 'Jesus' name'

Another incident similar to the one above happened 19 years ago. A member of the church was given only three days to live from a treatment that had gone wrong at the hands of the doctors. In the same way, all senior ministers had gone home after a long day in the office, and as I was set to leave, the phone rang and I answered.

Arriving the hospital, I was expected to offer the last prayers for the dying brother. Being too naïve, I commanded the demons to leave the man in the name of Jesus, instead of praying that God should pardon him and receive him into glory. The prayer of innocence said in the name of 'Jesus' has kept the brother alive until today.

HEALED, IN JESUS' NAME

ACTS 4:12

Nor is there salvation in any other, for there is no other name under heaven given among men by which we must be saved.

The word 'salvation' in the scripture above is translated 'health' in the King James Version of Acts 27:34. We would look at this later. The point here is that, there is no other name of which we can be healed except by the name of Jesus.

CHAPTER 3

Healing is God's Will

MATTHEW 8:2-3

And behold, a leper came and worshiped Him, saying, "Lord, if You are willing, You can make me clean." Then Jesus put out His hand and touched him, saying, "I am willing; be cleansed." Immediately his leprosy was cleansed.

MARK 1:40-42

Now a leper came to Him, imploring Him, kneeling down to Him and saying to Him, "If You are willing, You can make me clean." Then Jesus, moved with compassion, stretched out His hand and touched him, and said to him, "I am

HEALED, IN JESUS' NAME

willing; be cleansed." As soon as He had spoken, immediately the leprosy left him, and he was cleansed.

LUKE 5:12-13
And it happened when He was in a certain city, that behold, a man who was full of leprosy saw Jesus; and he fell on his face and implored Him, saying, "Lord, if You are willing, You can make me clean." Then He put out His hand and touched him, saying, "I am willing; be cleansed." Immediately the leprosy left him.

MATTHEW 6:10
Your kingdom come. Your will be done on earth as it is in heaven.

LUKE 11:2
So He said to them, "When you pray, say: Our Father in heaven, Hallowed be Your name. Your kingdom come. Your will be done On earth as it is in heaven.

REVELATIONS 21:4
And God will wipe away every tear from their eyes; there shall be no more death, nor sorrow, nor crying. There shall be no more pain, for the former things have passed away."

Chapter 3 - Healing is God's Will

In heaven, there is no sickness, diseases, infirmities or pain. If His will be done on earth as it is in heaven, then there should be no sickness, disease, infirmity or pain on earth.

PSALM 105:37
He also brought them out with silver and gold, and there was none feeble among His tribes.

When God brought His children out of darkness, He ensured that all weaknesses were removed.

MALACHI 4:2
But to you who fear my name, The Sun of Righteousness shall arise with healing in His wings; and you shall go out and grow fat like stall-fed calves.

For Christians, Christ will fly to our healing and we shall be well looked after, bodily.

MATTHEW 15:21-28
Then Jesus went out from there and departed to the region of Tyre and Sidon. And behold, a woman of Canaan came from that region and cried out to Him, saying, "Have mercy on me, O Lord, Son of David! My daughter is severely

demon-possessed." But He answered her not a word. And His disciples came and urged Him, saying, "Send her away, for she cries out after us." But He answered and said, "I was not sent except to the lost sheep of the house of Israel." Then she came and worshiped Him, saying, "Lord, help me!" But He answered and said, "It is not good to take the children's bread and throw it to the little dogs." And she said, "Yes, Lord, yet even the little dogs eat the crumbs which fall from their masters' table." Then Jesus answered and said to her, "O woman, great is your faith! Let it be to you as you desire." And her daughter was healed from that very hour.

SEE ALSO MARK 7:25-37

Healing is your right as a child of God. According to this scripture, it is the children's bread. It does not belong to the unrighteous; it is yours.

GALATIANS 3:13-14
Christ has redeemed us from the curse of the law, having become a curse for us (for it is written, "Cursed is everyone who hangs on a tree"), that the blessing of Abraham might come

Chapter 3 - Healing is God's Will

upon the Gentiles in Christ Jesus, that we might receive the promise of the Spirit through faith.

Christ has redeemed us from the curse of the law stated in Deuteronomy 28:15, 61.

LUKE 6:6-10
Now it happened on another Sabbath, also, that He entered the synagogue and taught. And a man was there whose right hand was withered. So the scribes and Pharisees watched Him closely, whether He would heal on the Sabbath, that they might find an accusation against Him. But He knew their thoughts, and said to the man who had the withered hand, "Arise and stand here." And he arose and stood. Then Jesus said to them, "I will ask you one thing: Is it lawful on the Sabbath to do good or to do evil, to save life or to destroy?" And when He had looked around at them all, He said to the man, "Stretch out your hand." And he did so, and his hand was restored as whole as the other.

LUKE 13:10-17
Now He was teaching in one of the synagogues on the Sabbath. And behold, there was a woman who had a spirit of infirmity eighteen years, and was bent over and could in no way raise herself

up. But when Jesus saw her, He called her to Him and said to her, "Woman, you are loosed from your infirmity." And He laid His hands on her, and immediately she was made straight, and glorified God. But the ruler of the synagogue answered with indignation, because Jesus had healed on the Sabbath; and he said to the crowd, "There are six days on which men ought to work; therefore come and be healed on them, and not on the Sabbath day." The Lord then answered him and said, "Hypocrite! Does not each one of you on the Sabbath loose his ox or donkey from the stall, and lead it away to water it? So ought not this woman, being a daughter of Abraham, whom Satan has bound—think of it—for eighteen years, be loosed from this bond on the Sabbath?" And when He said these things, all His adversaries were put to shame; and all the multitude rejoiced for all the glorious things that were done by Him.

JOHN 5:1-11

After this there was a feast of the Jews, and Jesus went up to Jerusalem. Now there is in Jerusalem by the Sheep Gate a pool, which is called in Hebrew, Bethesda, having five porches. In these lay a great multitude of sick people, blind, lame, paralyzed, waiting for the moving of the water. For an angel went down at a certain time into the

Chapter 3 - Healing is God's Will

pool and stirred up the water; then whoever stepped in first, after the stirring of the water, was made well of whatever disease he had. Now a certain man was there who had an infirmity thirty-eight years. When Jesus saw him lying there, and knew that he already had been in that condition a long time, He said to him, "Do you want to be made well?" The sick man answered Him, "Sir, I have no man to put me into the pool when the water is stirred up; but while I am coming, another steps down before me." Jesus said to him, "Rise, take up your bed and walk." And immediately the man was made well, took up his bed, and walked. And that day was the Sabbath. The Jews therefore said to him who was cured, "It is the Sabbath; it is not lawful for you to carry your bed." He answered them, "He who made me well said to me, 'Take up your bed and walk.' "

Jesus violated and overruled the Shabbat law in other to heal a man with a withered right hand, a woman who had a spirit of infirmity for eighteen years, and a crippled man just to prove a point; bodily healing is at the top of God's agenda and His will.

HEALED, IN JESUS' NAME

HEBREWS 4:14-16

Seeing then that we have a great High Priest who has passed through the heavens, Jesus the Son of God, let us hold fast our confession. For we do not have a High Priest who cannot sympathise with our weaknesses, but was in all points tempted as we are, yet without sin. Let us therefore come boldly to the throne of grace, that we may obtain mercy and find grace to help in time of need.

Christ knows what we feel and can relate to our suffering and He would not ignore or overlook our need.

3 JOHN 1:2

Beloved, I pray that you may prosper in all things and be in health, just as your soul prospers.

God wants you to do well (prosper) in all areas of life, including your health. If you exclude healing from salvation, salvation becomes incomplete.

The Greek words 'Soteria' translated 'salvation' and 'sozo' translated 'saved' included healing. 'Soteria' (so-tay-ree-a), Vines #4991

Chapter 3 - Healing is God's Will

means; rescue, safety, deliver, and health. 'Sozo' (sode'-zo), Vines #4982 means; to save, deliver or protect, to be made whole (in health, prosperity and peace of mind).

For example, in Acts 27:34 (KJV), the word translated 'health' is the Greek word 'Soteria.'

"Wherefore I pray you to take [some] meat: for this is for your health (Soteria): for there shall not an hair fall from the head of any of you."

Elsewhere, in the New Testament, 'Soteria' is translated 'Salvation' (Acts 4:12).

ROMANS 8:32
He who did not spare His own Son, but delivered Him up for us all, how shall He not with Him also freely give us all things?

God will not deny your healing because He did not withhold His Son. If He freely gave His most precious gift, in the person of Jesus, your healing is sure.

MATTHEW 7:7-11
"Ask, and it will be given to you; seek, and you will find; knock, and it will be opened to you.

For everyone who asks receives, and he who seeks finds, and to him who knocks it will be opened. Or what man is there among you who, if his son asks for bread, will give him a stone? Or if he asks for a fish, will he give him a serpent? If you then, being evil, know how to give good gifts to your children, how much more will your Father who is in heaven give good things to those who ask Him!

God wants to give us good gifts, including health and healing if we ask Him. If we, mortal men, can give good things to our children, God will do much more.

1 JOHN 5:14-15
Now this is the confidence that we have in Him, that if we ask anything according to His will, He hears us. And if we know that He hears us, whatever we ask, we know that we have the petitions that we have asked of Him.

Now that we know divine health and healing is the will of God, we can confidently pray to receive healing.

Chapter 3 - Healing is God's Will

Jesus came to give healing

EXODUS 15:26
And said, "If you diligently heed the voice of the LORD your God and do what is right in His sight, give ear to His commandments and keep all His statutes, I will put none of the diseases on you which I have brought on the Egyptians. For I am the LORD who heals you."

LUKE 9:56
For the Son of Man did not come to destroy men's lives but to save them. " And they went to another village.

JOHN 10:10
The thief does not come except to steal, and to kill, and to destroy. I have come that they may have life, and that they may have it more abundantly.

MATTHEW 12:15
But when Jesus knew it, He withdrew from there. And great multitudes followed Him, and He healed them all.

HEALED, IN JESUS' NAME

Christ still heals

HEBREWS 13:8
Jesus Christ is the same yesterday, today, and forever.

MALACHI 4:2
But to you who fear My name the Sun of Righteousness shall arise with healing in His wings; and you shall go out and grow fat like stall-fed calves.

ISAIAH 58:8 (speedy recovery)
Then your light shall break forth like the morning, your healing shall spring forth speedily, and your righteousness shall go before you; the glory of the Lord shall be your rear guard.

GENESIS 20:17
So Abraham prayed to God; and God healed Abimelech, his wife, and his female servants. Then they bore children.

2 CHRONICLES 30:20
And the Lord listened to Hezekiah and healed the people.

Chapter 3 - Healing is God's Will

2 KINGS 20:5

Return and tell Hezekiah the leader of My people, 'Thus says the Lord, the God of David your father: "I have heard your prayer, I have seen your tears; surely I will heal you. On the third day you shall go up to the house of the Lord."'

PSALM 6:2 & PSALM 30:2

Have mercy on me, O Lord, for I am weak; O Lord, heal me, for my bones are troubled. O LORD my God, I cried out to You, and You healed me.

HEALED, IN JESUS' NAME

CHAPTER 4

Diseases Have Spirits

2 CORINTHIANS 12:7

And lest I should be exalted above measure by the abundance of the revelations, a thorn in the flesh was given to me, a messenger of Satan to buffet me, lest I be exalted above measure.

- Paul's thorn in the flesh was a messenger of Satan. Cast out the demon and Paul would have been healed from his infirmity.

HEALED, IN JESUS' NAME

MATTHEW 8:16-17
When evening had come, they brought to Him many who were demon-possessed. And He cast out the spirits with a word, and healed all who were sick, that it might be fulfilled which was spoken by Isaiah the prophet, saying: "He Himself took our infirmities and bore our sicknesses."

- Jesus casts out the spirit and healed all who were sick

MATTHEW 9:31-34
But when they had departed, they spread the news about Him in all that country. As they went out, behold, they brought to Him a man, mute and demon-possessed. And when the demon was cast out, the mute spoke. And the multitudes marvelled, saying, "It was never seen like this in Israel!" But the Pharisees said, "He casts out demons by the ruler of the demons."

- When the demon was cast out, the mute spoke.

ACTS 10:38
How God anointed Jesus of Nazareth with the Holy Spirit and with power, who went about

Chapter 4 - Diseases Have Spirits

doing good and healing all who were oppressed by the devil, for God was with Him.

- Healing those who were oppressed by the devil.

ACTS 5:12-16
And through the hands of the apostles many signs and wonders were done among the people. And they were all with one accord in Solomon's Porch. Yet none of the rest dared join them, but the people esteemed them highly. And believers were increasingly added to the Lord, multitudes of both men and women, so that they brought the sick out into the streets and laid them on beds and couches, that at least the shadow of Peter passing by might fall on some of them. Also a multitude gathered from the surrounding cities to Jerusalem, bringing sick people and those who were tormented by unclean spirits, and they were all healed.

- Those who were sick and tormented by unclean spirits were all healed.

ACTS 8:5-8
Then Philip went down to the city of Samaria and preached Christ to them. And the

multitudes with one accord heeded the things spoken by Philip, hearing and seeing the miracles which he did. For unclean spirits, crying with a loud voice, came out of many who were possessed; and many who were paralysed and lame were healed. And there was great joy in that city.

- When the unclean spirits were cast out, the paralysed and lame were healed.

ACTS 19:11-12
Now God worked unusual miracles by the hands of Paul, so that even handkerchiefs or aprons were brought from his body to the sick, and the diseases left them and the evil spirits went out of them.

- When the sick were healed, the evil spirits left them.

LUKE 13:11-13
And behold, there was a woman who had a spirit of infirmity eighteen years, and was bent over and could in no way raise herself up. But when Jesus saw her, He called her to Him and said to her, "Woman, you are loosed from your infirmity." And He laid His hands on her, and

Chapter 4 - Diseases Have Spirits

immediately she was made straight, and glorified God.

- A woman had a spirit of infirmity. There is a spirit of infirmity.

MATTHEW 12:22
Then one was brought to Him who was demon-possessed, blind and mute; and He healed him, so that the blind and mute man both spoke and saw.

- The blind saw and the mute spoke when the demon-possessed was delivered.

LUKE 6:17-19
And He came down with them and stood on a level place with a crowd of His disciples and a great multitude of people from all Judea and Jerusalem, and from the seacoast of Tyre and Sidon, who came to hear Him and be healed of their diseases, as well as those who were tormented with unclean spirits. And they were healed. And the whole multitude sought to touch Him, for power went out from Him and healed them all.

HEALED, IN JESUS' NAME

- Jesus healed diseases and those who were tormented with unclean spirits.

MARK 5:8, 13, 15-16
For He said to him, "Come out of the man, unclean spirit!"

And at once Jesus gave them permission. Then the unclean spirits went out and entered the swine (there were about two thousand); and the herd ran violently down the steep place into the sea, and drowned in the sea.

Then they came to Jesus, and saw the one who had been demon-possessed and had the legion, sitting and clothed and in his right mind. And they were afraid. And those who saw it told them how it happened to him who had been demon-possessed, and about the swine.

- Spirit of an unclean spirit attached to mental disorder and madness.

MARK 9:17
Then one of the crowd answered and said, "Teacher, I brought You my son, who has a mute spirit.

Chapter 4 - Diseases Have Spirits

- Mute spirit is attached to being mute.

LUKE 4:33-36
Now in the synagogue there was a man who had a spirit of an unclean demon. And he cried out with a loud voice, saying, "Let us alone! What have we to do with You, Jesus of Nazareth? Did You come to destroy us? I know who You are—the Holy One of God!" But Jesus rebuked him, saying, "Be quiet, and come out of him!" And when the demon had thrown him in their midst, it came out of him and did not hurt him. Then they were all amazed and spoke among themselves, saying, "What a word this is! For with authority and power He commands the unclean spirits, and they come out."

- Spirit of an unclean demon attached to mental disorder and madness.

LUKE 4:40-41
When the sun was setting, all those who had any that were sick with various diseases brought them to Him; and He laid His hands on every one of them and healed them. And demons also came out of many, crying out and saying, "You are the Christ, the Son of God!" And He,

HEALED, IN JESUS' NAME

rebuking them, did not allow them to speak, for they knew that He was the Christ.

- Demons came out of many that were sick with various diseases and they were all healed.

CHAPTER 5

Sicknesses Are Transferred at Night

PSALM 91:5-6

You shall not be afraid of the terror by night, nor of the arrow that flies by day, nor of the pestilence that walks in darkness, nor of the destruction that lays waste at noonday.

The four periods of the day men are susceptible to attacks, according to the above scripture are, night, day, darkness and noonday. We would examine them one at a time.

Terror by Night

Night time is sleep time. This is usually between 6pm and 6am or in some countries, sunset to sunrise. Spiritual terrorism occurs in the night. As soon as the enemy discovers you are sleeping, he goes into action. The scripture says that Satan introduces terror by night.

Terrorism is defined as the unofficial and unauthorised use of violence and threats to intimidate or coerce, especially in the pursuit of political purposes. Terrorism creates fear, submission and surrender in the hearts of its subjects.

All nightmare experiences are handiworks of Satan. If you find a hefty man suddenly waking up from sleep sweating and perspiring heavily during winter, the terrorist has visited him.

Other signs of terrorist actions during sleep include but not limited to the following:

- Sleep Paralysis - this is the inability to perform voluntary muscular movement during sleep which some people might describe as a feeling of being held down in a dream or sleep or when you are just waking up generally known as ISP (Isolated Sleep Paralysis)

Chapter 5 - Sicknesses Are Transferred At Night

or RISP (Recurrent Isolated Sleep Paralysis).

- Chase Dreams - includes being pursued by dangerous snakes, killer dogs, and other animals.
- Death dreams - includes gunshots, knife attacks, car accidents, plane crash, drowning, and the likes.
- Violated Dreams - rape, abuses or oppressions, being cheated or robbed, bags snatched, kidnap, etc.
- Falling Dreams - from a hill, tree, ladder, rooftop, aircraft, cliff and the likes

In the Hebrew, 'pachad' is translated terror. It occurs 40 out of 49 times to mean 'fear'. We can, therefore, conclude that terror is to induce fear. When a man experiences fear at night or during sleep, he has been visited by Satan.

Arrows by day

PSALM 64:3, NASB
Who have sharpened their tongue like a sword. They aimed bitter speech as their arrow.

HEALED, IN JESUS' NAME

PROVERBS 25:18
A man who bears false witness against his neighbour is like a club, a sword, and a sharp arrow.

JEREMIAH 9:8
Their tongue is an arrow shot out; it speaks deceit; one speaks peaceably to his neighbour with his mouth, but in his heart he lies in wait.

EZEKIEL 5:16
When I send against them the terrible arrows of famine which shall be for destruction, which I will send to destroy you, I will increase the famine upon you and cut off your supply of bread.

PSALM 57:4
My soul is among lions; I lie among the sons of men who are set on fire, whose teeth are spears and arrows, and their tongue a sharp sword.

From the passages above, we find that arrows that fly by day include arrows of hatred, lies, malice, rejection, abuses, curses, bitterness, sickness, poverty and lack. The vehicle of inflicting the arrows is the mouth, lips or words, our utterances and confessions.

Chapter 5 - Sicknesses Are Transferred At Night

The day is the hours between sunrise and sunset, usually between 6am and 6pm.

To deal with arrows, we use the following scriptures:

ISAIAH 54:17
No weapon formed against you shall prosper, and every tongue which rises against you in judgment You shall condemn. This is the heritage of the servants of the LORD, and their righteousness is from Me," says the LORD.

PSALM 58:7
Let them flow away as waters which run continually; when he bends his bow, let his arrows be as if cut in pieces.

EPHESIANS 6:16, NASB
In addition to all, taking up the shield of faith with which you will be able to extinguish all the flaming arrows of the evil one.

Pestilence in darkness

The night is between sunset and sunrise (6pm-6am). However, darkness is between 12 midnight and dawn. To be more precise, night represents the hours between 12 midnight and 3am. 12 midnight is 'witching hour'. So is 12 noon.

How strategic it would be for believers to pray between the hours of 12 midnight and 3 am when sicknesses and diseases are being distributed?

Pestilence is defined and described as deadly epidemic diseases. Through the verse of scripture, pestilence is the only diseases related to the affliction of the devil. We, therefore, conclude that pestilence covers illnesses, sicknesses and diseases. The scriptures also tell us that these pestilences walk in darkness. Walking signifies that they are constantly on the move, seeking potential hosts and a permanent place of abode.

As an unsaved 'religious' person, I would dream of some strange individual whipping me with the African broom during sleep. When I would wake up, you could notice marks on my body. However, since I became a Christian, the devil activities were refused, and I am now free.

All forms of heart problems, liver problems, kidneys, lungs, skin diseases, stomach pains, blood diseases, viral infections, lumps and tumours, the list goes on, are distributed in darkness.

Chapter 5 - Sicknesses Are Transferred At Night

Instead of waking up refreshed, people wake up either coughing, sneezing, feverish or with cancer, arthritis, migraine. The joint pains, the headaches, the swelling and tiredness are common with people when they wake up.

Noonday Destruction

Going back to our text, we read,

PSALM 91:5-6
You shall not be afraid of the terror by night, nor of the arrow that flies by day, nor of the pestilence that walks in darkness, nor of the destruction that lays waste at noonday.

There are a couple of points I want to make.

First, to lay waste is to lay an ambush, secretly watching for an opportune time. The devil usually does want to catch his prey unawares. He is patient and not in a hurry.

Secondly, the noonday is a period of the day between 12 noon and 6 pm. However, the hours between 3 pm and 6 pm are the most delicate hours of the busy day. You would notice that people are agitated and tensed after a hard day at work. The outcome is to snap at the spouse or children and anyone at home. The person is upset for no reason giving the devil the much-anticipated advantage. This attitude is self-destructive. Such an individual would do well to heed Apostle Paul's warning,

EPHESIANS 4:26-27
Be angry, and do not sin": do not let the sun go down on your wrath, nor give place to the devil.

As we can see, sicknesses are transferred in the night.

CHAPTER 6

Causes of Sicknesses

Sickness is not from God

GENESIS 1:25

And God made the beast of the earth according to its kind, cattle according to its kind, and everything that creeps on the earth according to its kind. And God saw that it was good.

JAMES 1:16-17

Do not be deceived, my beloved brethren. Every good gift and every perfect gift is from above, and comes down from the Father of lights, with whom there is no variation or shadow of turning.

ACTS 10:38
How God anointed Jesus of Nazareth with the Holy Spirit and with power, who went about doing good and healing all who were oppressed by the devil, for God was with Him.

EXODUS 15:26
And said, "If you diligently heed the voice of the LORD your God and do what is right in His sight, give ear to His commandments and keep all His statutes, I will put none of the diseases on you which I have brought on the Egyptians. For I am the LORD who heals you."

ISAIAH 53:4-5
Surely He has borne our griefs and carried our sorrows; yet we esteemed Him stricken, smitten by God, and afflicted. But He was wounded for our transgressions, He was bruised for our iniquities; the chastisement for our peace was upon Him, and by His stripes we are healed.

1 PETER 2:24
who Himself bore our sins in His own body on the tree, that we, having died to sins, might live

Chapter 6 - Causes of Sicknesses

for righteousness— by whose stripes you were healed. (I Peter 2:24 NKJV)

MATTHEW 8:16-17
When evening had come, they brought to Him many who were demon-possessed. And He cast out the spirits with a word, and healed all who were sick, that it might be fulfilled which was spoken by Isaiah the prophet, saying: "He Himself took our infirmities and bore our sicknesses."

JOHN 10:10
The thief does not come except to steal, and to kill, and to destroy. I have come that they may have life, and that they may have it more abundantly.

Sickness is from the Devil

JOB 2:7-8
So Satan went out from the presence of the LORD, and struck Job with painful boils from the sole of his foot to the crown of his head. And he took for himself a potsherd with which to scrape himself while he sat in the midst of the ashes.

HEALED, IN JESUS' NAME

2 CORINTHIANS 12:7
And lest I should be exalted above measure by the abundance of the revelations, a thorn in the flesh was given to me, a messenger of Satan to buffet me, lest I be exalted above measure.

ACTS 10:38
How God anointed Jesus of Nazareth with the Holy Spirit and with power, who went about doing good and healing all who were oppressed by the devil, for God was with Him.

MATTHEW 12:22
Then one was brought to Him who was demon-possessed, blind and mute; and He healed him, so that the blind and mute man both spoke and saw.

Sickness is a result of fallen human nature

Environmental factors can contribute to diseases (as distinct from infection and genetic factors). In those predisposed to a particular genetic condition, environmental risk factors can precipitate the unset or the manifestation of the underlying diseased state apart from the true monogenic genetic disorders. Substances and

Chapter 6 - Causes of Sicknesses

chemicals found in household cleaners and in almost all personal care products added to stress, physical and mental abuse, diet, exposure to toxins, pathogens, radiation are possible causes of a large segment of non-hereditary diseases.

A WHO's report shows how specific diseases are influenced by environmental risks and by how much.[1]

As much as 24% of global disease is caused by environmental exposures which can be averted. It is estimated that environmental exposures cause more than 33% of disease in children under the age of 5. The estimate reflects how much death, illness and disability could be realistically avoided every year as a result of better environmental management.

The report estimates that more than 13 million deaths annually are due to preventable environmental causes. Nearly one-third of death and disease in the least developed regions is due to environmental causes. Over 40% of deaths from malaria and an estimated 94% of deaths from diarrhoeal diseases, two of the world's biggest childhood killers, could be prevented through better environmental management. The four main diseases influenced by poor environments are diarrhoea, lower respiratory infections, various forms of unintentional injuries, and malaria.

Diseases with the largest total annual health burden from environmental factors, in terms of death, illness and disability or Disability Adjusted Life Years (DALYs) are:

- Diarrhoea (58 million DALYS per year; 94% of the diarrhoeal burden of disease) largely from unsafe water, sanitation and hygiene
- Lower respiratory infections (37 million DALYs per year; 41% of all cases globally) largely from air pollution, indoor and outdoor.
- Malaria (19 million DALYs per year; 42% of all cases globally), largely as a result of poor water resource, housing and land use management which fails to curb vector populations effectively.
- Chronic Obstructive Pulmonary Disease (COPD) -- a slowly progressing disease characterized by a gradual loss of lung function. (COPD, 12 million DALYs per year; 42% of all cases globally) largely as a result of exposures to workplace dust and

Chapter 6 - Causes of Sicknesses

fumes and other forms of indoor and outdoor air pollution.

- Perinatal conditions (11 million DALYS per year; 11% of all cases globally).
- Most of the same environmentally triggered diseases also rank as the biggest killers outright -- although they rank somewhat differently in order of lethality. Diseases with the largest absolute number of deaths annually from modifiable environmental factors (these are all parts of the environment amenable to change using available technologies, policies, preventive and public health measure). These diseases include:

- 2.6 million deaths annually from cardiovascular diseases
- 1.7 million deaths annually from diarrhoeal diseases
- 1.5 million deaths annually from lower respiratory infections
- 1.4 million deaths annually from cancers, including skin cancer caused by excessive exposure to ultraviolet radiation in sunlight

- 1.3 million deaths annually from chronic obstructive Pulmonary disease

The report shows that one way or another, the environment significantly affects more than 80% of these major diseases.

[1]WHO | Almost a quarter of all disease caused by environmental exposure, http://www.who.int/mediacentre/news/releases/2006/pr32/en/ (accessed May 07, 2015).

Sickness is from life choices

- Cigarettes - cancer, lungs diseases
- Alcohol - causes diseases across almost all the major organs in the body affecting the heart, liver, blood vessels and other organs resulting in impotence, hypertension etc. and its implicated in majority of cancers
- Fornication or marital unfaithfulness - sexually transmitted infections (STI) or HIV/AIDS or Hepatitis B and C
- Fatty or high sugary foods - Cardiovascular (heart and blood vessels)

Chapter 6 - Causes of Sicknesses

- Using recreational or illicit drugs - emotional fluctuations, anger outburst, poor sleep, depression, anxiety, psychosis, panic attacks etc.
- Body piercing or tattoos - Hepatitis B and C or HIV/AIDS

Sickness caused as a result of sin and disobedience

The following describes the consequences of disobedience and not the personality of God. When the Bible implied an evil act as coming from God, it means that God when He withdraws His protection from a man, the enemy would have free access to that man's life. The case of Job typifies those of many others typifies. God is a good God, and there is no evil in Him.

JAMES 5:14-16

Is anyone among you sick? Let him call for the elders of the church, and let them pray over him, anointing him with oil in the name of the Lord. And the prayer of faith will save the sick, and the Lord will raise him up. And if he has committed sins, he will be forgiven. Confess your trespasses to one another, and pray for one another, that you may be healed. The effective, fervent prayer of a righteous man avails much.

PSALM 25:18
Look on my affliction and my pain, and forgive all my sins.

PSALM 103:3
Bless the LORD, O my soul, and forget not all His benefits: Who forgives all your iniquities, Who heals all your diseases.

2 CHRONICLES 7:14
If My people who are called by My name will humble themselves, and pray and seek My face, and turn from their wicked ways, then I will hear from heaven, and will forgive their sin and heal their land.

LUKE 5:17-25 (MARK 2:1-12)
Now it happened on a certain day, as He was teaching, that there were Pharisees and teachers of the law sitting by, who had come out of every town of Galilee, Judea, and Jerusalem. And the power of the Lord was present to heal them. Then behold, men brought on a bed a man who was paralysed, whom they sought to bring in

Chapter 6 - Causes of Sicknesses

and lay before Him. And when they could not find how they might bring him in, because of the crowd, they went up on the housetop and let him down with his bed through the tiling into the midst before Jesus. When He saw their faith, He said to him, "Man, your sins are forgiven you." And the scribes and the Pharisees began to reason, saying, "Who is this who speaks blasphemies? Who can forgive sins but God alone?" But when Jesus perceived their thoughts, He answered and said to them, "Why are you reasoning in your hearts? Which is easier, to say, 'Your sins are forgiven you,' or to say, 'Rise up and walk'? But that you may know that the Son of Man has power on earth to forgive sins" — He said to the man who was paralysed, "I say to you, arise, take up your bed, and go to your house." Immediately he rose up before them, took up what he had been lying on, and departed to his own house, glorifying God.

JOHN 9:1-7

Now as Jesus passed by, He saw a man who was blind from birth. And His disciples asked Him, saying, "Rabbi, who sinned, this man or his parents, that he was born blind?" Jesus answered, "Neither this man nor his parents sinned, but that the works of God should be revealed in him. I must work the works of Him who sent Me while it is day; the night is coming when no one can work. As long as I am in the world, I am the light of the world." When He had said these things, He spat on the ground and made clay with the saliva; and He anointed the eyes of the blind man with the clay. And He said to him, "Go, wash in the pool of Siloam" (which is translated, Sent). So he went and washed, and came back seeing.

DEUTERONOMY 28:15, 21 (curse of the law)

But it shall come to pass, if you do not obey the voice of the LORD your God, to observe carefully all His commandments and His statutes which I command you today, that all these curses will come upon you and overtake you: The LORD will make the plague cling to you until He has consumed you from the land which you are going to possess.

DEUTERONOMY 28:21

The LORD will make the plague cling to you until He has consumed you from the land which you are going to possess.

- Plagues (also known as diseases)

Chapter 6 - Causes of Sicknesses

DEUTERONOMY 28:22

The LORD will strike you with consumption, with fever, with inflammation, with severe burning fever, with the sword, with scorching, and with mildew; they shall pursue you until you perish.

- Consumption (Wasting diseases - cancer; Alzheimer's dementia; etc. including all types of muscular dystrophy and neuromuscular diseases),
- Inflammations (cold; ague or malaria fever; infections),
- Severe burning fever (influenza; sunstroke; erysipelas, the infectious disease of the hands),
- Scorching (blight),
- Mildew (jaundice; paleness).

DEUTERONOMY 28:27

The LORD will strike you with the boils of Egypt, with tumours, with the scab, and with the itch, from which you cannot be healed.

- Boils of Egypt (inflammatory disease; ulcers; sores),

- Tumours or Emerods (haemorrhoids; ulcers; swellings in the groin, e.g. hernias; sores),
- Scab (eczema; incurable itch; malignant scab; festering sores; and scurvy - a vitamin c deficiency, which can also lead to anaemia, debility, exhaustion, oedema, and sometimes ulceration of the gums and loss of teeth),
- The Itch (incurable itch and other sorts of skin diseases)

DEUTERONOMY 28:28

The LORD will strike you with madness and blindness and confusion of heart.

- Madness (insanity; loss of mind; mind diseases),
- Blindness
- Confusion of heart (confusion of distraction of mind; imbecility; dismay of mind and heart; crazed wits; panic attacks),

DEUTERONOMY 28:35

The LORD will strike you in the knees and on the legs with severe boils which cannot be

Chapter 6 - Causes of Sicknesses

healed, and from the sole of your foot to the top of your head.

- Severe boils which cannot be healed (i.e. boils, carbuncles and furunculosis all over the body from the sole of foot to the top of head).

DEUTERONOMY 28:59
Then the LORD will bring upon you and your descendants extraordinary plagues—great and prolonged plagues—and serious and prolonged sicknesses.

- Hereditary, malignant diseases (cancers, high blood pressure, diabetes, and all genetic disorders),
- Prolonged sicknesses (migraine, the Epstein-Barr virus or EBV, also called human herpesvirus 4 or HHV-4 causing glandular fevers; cytomegalovirus infection; strokes; epidemics etc.)

DEUTERONOMY 28:60
Moreover He will bring back on you all the diseases of Egypt, of which you were afraid, and they shall cling to you.

HEALED, IN JESUS' NAME

- All foreign diseases

DEUTERONOMY 28:61
Also every sickness and every plague, which is not written in this Book of the Law, will the LORD bring upon you until you are destroyed.

- Strange and new (uncategorised) sicknesses and diseases

Sickness caused by unforgiveness

It can hinder someone's reactions to treatments or even the willingness to pursue treatment. Unforgiveness makes and keeps people sick.

PSALM 147:3
He heals the broken-hearted and binds up their wounds.

- Emotional Wounds and Disorders
- Cancer - It's classified as a disease in medical books and Forgiveness Therapy is used in the treatment of cancer. 61% of all cancer patients have

Chapter 6 - Causes of Sicknesses

forgiveness issues and half of these are severe. These negative emotions (anger and hatred) create a state of chronic anxiety which produces adrenalin and cortisol which depletes the production of natural killer cells, which are the body's foot soldiers to fight cancer.[1]

[1] Dr. Steven Standiford, Cancer Treatment Surgeon, Certified Therapeutic Recreation Specialist (CTRS) of America. Dr. Michael S. Barry, Pastor and Author, "The Forgiveness Project"

# HEALED, IN JESUS' NAME

CHAPTER 7

Documented Healing in the New Testament

Ministry of Jesus

- All manner of sicknesses and diseases - Matthew 4:23-24; 8:16-17; 9:35; 12:15; 14:14, 34-36; 15:30-31; Mark 6:53-56; Luke 4:40-41; 5:15; 6:17-19; Acts 10:38
- Blindness - Matthew 9:27-31; 12:22; 15:29-31; 20:29-34; Mark 8:22-25; Luke 18:35-43; John 9:1-11
- Bowed down - Luke 13:10-17

HEALED, IN JESUS' NAME

- Crippled (Impotence in feet) - John 5:1-14
- Dead raised - Luke 7:11-16; Luke 8:49-56; John 11:1-44
- Deafness - Mark 7:31-37
- Demonised - Matthew 4:23-24; Matthew 8:16-17
- Dropsy Luke 14:1-5
- Dumbness/Mute - Matthew 9:31-34; 12:22; 15:29-31; Mark 7:31-37; 9:17-29; Luke 11:5-14
- Epileptic - Luke 9:37-43
- Fever - Matthew 8:14-15; Mark 1:29-34
- Haemorrhage - Matthew 9:18-22; Mark 5:25-34; Luke 8:43-48
- Lame - Matthew 15:29-31
- Leprosy - Matthew 8:2-3; Mark 1:40-42; Luke 5:12-14; 17:11-19
- Maimed - Matthew 15:29-31
- Mental disorder and madness - Mark 5:1-20; Luke 4:33-36
- Nobleman's son healed John 4:45-53
- Palsy/Paralytic - Matthew 8:5-10, 13; Luke 5:17-25

Chapter 7 - Documented Healing in The New Testament

- Terminal disease - Luke 7:1-10
- Unclean Spirit - Mark 7:24-30; Luke 4:31-36
- Withered hand - Matthew 12:9-13; Luke 6:6-10

Ministry of the Apostles and Disciples

- All manner of sicknesses and diseases - Mark 6:7, 12-13; 16:15-20; Luke 9:1-2, 6; Acts 5:12-16; 6:8; 8:5-8; 19:11-12; 28:8-9
- Crippled (Impotence in feet) - Acts 14:8-10
- Fever - Acts 28:8-9
- Haemorrhage - Acts 28:8-9
- Lameness - Acts 3:1-10;
- Palsy - Acts 9:32-34

HEALED, IN JESUS' NAME

CHAPTER 8

Healed, In Jesus' Name

There is no other name that can work such wonders; except the name of Jesus. As far as under heaven (earth and under the earth) is concerned, the only name commanding surrender and capitulation is the name of Jesus.

PHILIPPIANS 2:9-11
Therefore God also has highly exalted Him and given Him the name which is above every name, that at the name of Jesus every knee should bow, of those in heaven, and of those on earth, and of those under the earth, and that every tongue should confess that Jesus Christ is Lord, to the glory of God the Father.

HEALED, IN JESUS' NAME

ACTS 4:12
Nor is there salvation in any other, for there is no other name under heaven given among men by which we must be saved.

JOHN 14:12-14
Most assuredly, I say to you, he who believes in Me, the works that I do he will do also; and greater works than these he will do, because I go to My Father. And whatever you ask in My name, that I will do, that the Father may be glorified in the Son. If you ask anything in My name, I will do it.

JOHN 15:16
You did not choose Me, but I chose you and appointed you that you should go and bear fruit, and that your fruit should remain, that whatever you ask the Father in My name He may give you.

JOHN 16:23-24
And in that day you will ask Me nothing. Most assuredly, I say to you, whatever you ask the Father in My name He will give you. Until now you have asked nothing in My name. Ask, and you will receive, that your joy may be full.

Chapter 8 - Healed, In Jesus' name

ACTS 4:9-10

If we this day are judged for a good deed done to a helpless man, by what means he has been made well, let it be known to you all, and to all the people of Israel, that by the name of Jesus Christ of Nazareth, whom you crucified, whom God raised from the dead, by Him this man stands here before you whole.

ACTS 4:29-30

Now, Lord, look on their threats, and grant to Your servants that with all boldness they may speak Your word, by stretching out Your hand to heal, and that signs and wonders may be done through the name of Your holy Servant Jesus.

There is authority in the name of Jesus

MATTHEW 28:18-19

And Jesus came and spoke to them, saying, "All authority has been given to Me in heaven and on earth. Go therefore and make disciples of all the nations, baptizing them in the name of the Father and of the Son and of the Holy Spirit.

HEALED, IN JESUS' NAME

LUKE 10:19
Behold, I give you the authority to trample on serpents and scorpions, and over all the power of the enemy, and nothing shall by any means hurt you.

MARK 16:17-18
And these signs will follow those who believe: In My name they will cast out demons; they will speak with new tongues; they will take up serpents; and if they drink anything deadly, it will by no means hurt them; they will lay hands on the sick, and they will recover.

Believers have the power over the Devil and the right to use the name of Jesus

COLOSSIANS 2:13-15
And you, being dead in your trespasses and the uncircumcision of your flesh, He has made alive together with Him, having forgiven you all trespasses, having wiped out the handwriting of requirements that was against us, which was contrary to us. And He has taken it out of the way, having nailed it to the cross. Having disarmed principalities and powers, He made a

Chapter 8 - Healed, In Jesus' name

public spectacle of them, triumphing over them in it.

MATTHEW 28:18-19
And Jesus came and spoke to them, saying, "All authority has been given to Me in heaven and on earth. Go therefore and make disciples of all the nations, baptising them in the name of the Father and of the Son and of the Holy Spirit."

MARK 16:17-18
And these signs will follow those who believe: In My name they will cast out demons; they will speak with new tongues; they will take up serpents; and if they drink anything deadly, it will by no means hurt them; they will lay hands on the sick, and they will recover."

MATTHEW 8:5-10
Now when Jesus had entered Capernaum, a centurion came to Him, pleading with Him, saying, "Lord, my servant is lying at home paralysed, dreadfully tormented." And Jesus said to him, "I will come and heal him." The centurion answered and said, "Lord, I am not worthy that You should come under my roof. But only speak a word, and my servant will be healed. For I also am a man under authority,

having soldiers under me. And I say to this one, 'Go,' and he goes; and to another, 'Come,' and he comes; and to my servant, 'Do this,' and he does it." When Jesus heard it, He marvelled, and said to those who followed, "Assuredly, I say to you, I have not found such great faith, not even in Israel!

John 3:14-15
And as Moses lifted up the serpent in the wilderness, even so must the Son of Man be lifted up, that whoever believes in Him should not perish but have eternal life.

Demons will not obey unbelievers

ACTS 19:13-16
Then some of the itinerant Jewish exorcists took it upon themselves to call the name of the Lord Jesus over those who had evil spirits, saying, "We exorcise you by the Jesus whom Paul preaches." Also there were seven sons of Sceva, a Jewish chief priest, who did so. And the evil spirit answered and said, "Jesus I know, and Paul I know; but who are you?" Then the man in whom the evil spirit was leaped on them, overpowered[b] them, and prevailed against

Chapter 8 - Healed, In Jesus' name

them, so that they fled out of that house naked and wounded.

Healings follow the use of the name of Jesus

JOHN 14:12-14
Most assuredly, I say to you, he who believes in Me, the works that I do he will do also; and greater works than these he will do, because I go to My Father. And whatever you ask in My name, that I will do, that the Father may be glorified in the Son. If you ask anything in My name, I will do it.

MARK 16:15-20
And He said to them, "Go into all the world and preach the gospel to every creature. He who believes and is baptised will be saved; but he who does not believe will be condemned. And these signs will follow those who believe: In My name they will cast out demons; they will speak with new tongues; they will take up serpents; and if they drink anything deadly, it will by no means hurt them; they will lay hands on the sick, and they will recover." So then, after the Lord had spoken to them, He was received up into heaven, and sat down at the right hand of God.

HEALED, IN JESUS' NAME

And they went out and preached everywhere, the Lord working with them and confirming the word through the accompanying signs. Amen

ACTS 3:6, 16
Then Peter said, "Silver and gold I do not have, but what I do have I give you: In the name of Jesus Christ of Nazareth, rise up and walk." And His name, through faith in His name, has made this man strong, whom you see and know. Yes, the faith which comes through Him has given him this perfect soundness in the presence of you all.

CHAPTER 9

Healing Scriptures

The healing Scriptures are based on Christ's finished work of Calvary and promises of God in His word.

GALATIANS 3:13-14
Christ has redeemed us from the curse of the law, having become a curse for us (for it is written, "Cursed is everyone who hangs on a tree"), that the blessing of Abraham might come upon the Gentiles in Christ Jesus, that we might receive the promise of the Spirit through faith.

ISAIAH 53:4-5

Surely He has borne our griefs and carried our sorrows; yet we esteemed Him stricken, smitten by God, and afflicted. But He was wounded for our transgressions, He was bruised for our iniquities; the chastisement for our peace was upon Him, and by His stripes we are healed.

MATTHEW 8:16-17

When evening had come, they brought to Him many who were demon-possessed. And He cast out the spirits with a word, and healed all who were sick, that it might be fulfilled which was spoken by Isaiah the prophet, saying: "He Himself took our infirmities and bore our sicknesses."

ROMANS 8:2

For the law of the Spirit of life in Christ Jesus has made me free from the law of sin and death.

ROMANS 8:11

But if the Spirit of Him who raised Jesus from the dead dwells in you, He who raised Christ from the dead will also give life to your mortal bodies through His Spirit who dwells in you.

Chapter 9 - Healing Scriptures

1 PETER 2:24
Who Himself bore our sins in His own body on the tree, that we, having died to sins, might live for righteousness—by whose stripes you were healed.

1 JOHN 3:8
He who sins is of the devil, for the devil has sinned from the beginning. For this purpose the Son of God was manifested, that He might destroy the works of the devil.

3 JOHN 2
Beloved, I pray that you may prosper in all things and be in health, just as your soul prospers.

Healing of the soul (the greatest miracle)

MARK 16:15-18
And He said to them, "Go into all the world and preach the gospel to every creature. He who believes and is baptised will be saved; but he who does not believe will be condemned. And these signs will follow those who believe: In My name they will cast out demons; they will speak with new tongues; they will take up serpents;

and if they drink anything deadly, it will by no means hurt them; they will lay hands on the sick, and they will recover."

LUKE 10:17-20

Then the seventy returned with joy, saying, "Lord, even the demons are subject to us in Your name." And He said to them, "I saw Satan fall like lightning from heaven. Behold, I give you the authority to trample on serpents and scorpions, and over all the power of the enemy, and nothing shall by any means hurt you. Nevertheless do not rejoice in this, that the spirits are subject to you, but rather rejoice because your names are written in heaven."

ROMANS 10:9-10

That if you confess with your mouth the Lord Jesus and believe in your heart that God has raised Him from the dead, you will be saved. For with the heart one believes unto righteousness, and with the mouth confession is made unto salvation.

Chapter 9 - Healing Scriptures

Abdominal Pain/Ache

PROVERBS 18:20
A man's stomach shall be satisfied from the fruit of his mouth; *from* the produce of his lips he shall be filled.

SONG OF SOLOMON 7:2
Your navel *is* a rounded goblet; it lacks no blended beverage. Your waist *is* a heap of wheat set about with lilies.

ACTS 28:7-8
In that region there was an estate of the leading citizen of the island, whose name was Publius, who received us and entertained us courteously for three days. And it happened that the father of Publius lay sick of a fever and dysentery. Paul went in to him and prayed, and he laid his hands on him and healed him.

Arms and Hands

NEHEMIAH 6:9
For they all *were trying to* make us afraid, saying, "Their hands will be weakened in the work, and

it will not be done." Now therefore, *O God*, strengthen my hands.

PSALM 18:34
He teaches my hands to make war, so that my arms can bend a bow of bronze.

PSALM 34:19-20
Many are the afflictions of the righteous, but the LORD delivers him out of them all. He guards all his bones; not one of them is broken.

PSALM 144:1
Blessed *be* the LORD my Rock, Who trains my hands for war, a*nd* my fingers for battle.

HOSEA 7:15
Though I disciplined *and* strengthened their arms, yet they devise evil against Me.

MARK 3:3-5
And He said to the man who had the withered hand, "Step forward." Then He said to them, "Is it lawful on the Sabbath to do good or to do evil, to save life or to kill?" But they kept silent. And when He had looked around at them with anger, being grieved by the hardness of their hearts, He

said to the man, "Stretch out your hand." And he stretched *it* out, and his hand was restored as whole as the other.

Arthritis

JOB 4:3-4
Surely you have instructed many, and you have strengthened weak hands. Your words have upheld him who was stumbling, and you have strengthened the feeble knees.

PSALM 145:14
The Lord upholds all who fall, and raises up all who are bowed down.

PSALM 146:8
The Lord opens the eyes of the blind; The Lord raises those who are bowed down; The Lord loves the righteous.

PSALM 105:37
He also brought them out with silver and gold, and there was none feeble among His tribes.

PROVERBS 3:7-8
Do not be wise in your own eyes; fear the Lord and depart from evil. It will be health to your flesh, and strength to your bones.

SONG OF SOLOMON 5:15
His legs *are* pillars of marble set on bases of fine gold. His countenance *is* like Lebanon, excellent as the cedars.

SONG OF SOLOMON 7:1
How beautiful are your feet in sandals, O prince's daughter! The curves of your thighs *are* like jewels, the work of the hands of a skillful workman.

ISAIAH 35:3
Strengthen the weak hands, and make firm the feeble knees.

JOEL 3:9-10
Proclaim this among the nations: "Prepare for war! Wake up the mighty men, let all the men of war draw near, Let them come up. Beat your ploughshares into swords and your pruning hooks into spears; Let the weak say, 'I am strong.'"

Chapter 9 - Healing Scriptures

HEBREWS 12:12-13
Therefore strengthen the hands which hang down, and the feeble knees, and make straight paths for your feet, so that what is lame may not be dislocated, but rather be healed.

Asthma and Breathing Problems

PSALM 91:3
Surely He shall deliver you from the snare of the fowler and from the perilous pestilence.

ISAIAH 42:5
Thus says God the LORD, Who created the heavens and stretched them out, Who spread forth the earth and that which comes from it, Who gives breath to the people on it, and spirit to those who walk on it.

EZEKIEL 37:5
Thus says the Lord GOD to these bones: "Surely I will cause breath to enter into you, and you shall live.

HEALED, IN JESUS' NAME

ACTS 17:25
Nor is He worshiped with men's hands, as though He needed anything, since He gives to all life, breath, and all things.

Barrenness

GENESIS 18:14
Is anything too hard for the Lord? At the appointed time I will return to you, according to the time of life, and Sarah shall have a son."

DEUTERONOMY 7:12-15 (BLESSING OF OBEDIENCE)
Then it shall come to pass, because you listen to these judgments, and keep and do them, that the Lord your God will keep with you the covenant and the mercy which He swore to your fathers. And He will love you and bless you and multiply you; He will also bless the fruit of your womb and the fruit of your land, your grain and your new wine and your oil, the increase of your cattle and the offspring of your flock, in the land of which He swore to your fathers to give you. You shall be blessed above all peoples; there shall not be a male or female barren among you or among your livestock. And the Lord will take

Chapter 9 - Healing Scriptures

away from you all sickness, and will afflict you with none of the terrible diseases of Egypt which you have known, but will lay them on all those who hate you.

PSALM 113:9
He grants the barren woman a home, like a joyful mother of children. Praise the Lord!

ISAIAH 66:7
Before she was in labor, she gave birth; before her pain came, she delivered a male child.

1 TIMOTHY 2:15
Nevertheless she will be saved in childbearing if they continue in faith, love, and holiness, with self-control.

Blood Diseases, High Blood Pressure, Anaemia, Leukaemia, Diabetes

PSALM 138:7
Though I walk in the midst of trouble, You will revive me; You will stretch out Your hand against the wrath of my enemies, and Your right hand will save me.

HEALED, IN JESUS' NAME

EZEKIEL 16:6
And when I passed by you and saw you struggling in your own blood, I said to you in your blood, 'Live!' Yes, I said to you in your blood, 'Live!'

JOEL 3:21
For I will acquit them of the guilt of bloodshed, whom I had not acquitted; for the Lord dwells in Zion.

MATTHEW 9:20-22
And suddenly, a woman who had a flow of blood for twelve years came from behind and touched the hem of His garment. For she said to herself, "If only I may touch His garment, I shall be made well." But Jesus turned around, and when He saw her He said, "Be of good cheer, daughter; your faith has made you well." And the woman was made well from that hour.

MARK 5:29
Now a certain woman had a flow of blood for twelve years, and had suffered many things from many physicians. She had spent all that she had and was no better, but rather grew worse. When she heard about Jesus, she came behind *Him* in the crowd and touched His garment. For

Chapter 9 - Healing Scriptures

she said, "If only I may touch His clothes, I shall be made well." Immediately the fountain of her blood was dried up, and she felt in *her* body that she was healed of the affliction.

1 CORINTHIAN 3:16
Do you not know that you are the temple of God and that the Spirit of God dwells in you?

Bed Wetting

PSALM 144:7
Stretch out Your hand from above; rescue me and deliver me out of great waters, from the hand of foreigners.

MATTHEW 8:17
That it might be fulfilled which was spoken by Isaiah the prophet, saying: "He Himself took our infirmities and bore our sicknesses."

Bone and Back Problems

PSALM 6:2
Have mercy on me, O Lord, for I *am* weak; O Lord, heal me, for my bones are troubled.

HEALED, IN JESUS' NAME

PSALM 25:20
Keep my soul, and deliver me; let me not be ashamed, for I put my trust in You.

PSALM 34:20
He guards all his bones; not one of them is broken.

PSALM 92:14
They shall still bear fruit in old age; they shall be fresh and flourishing.

PROVERBS 3:8
It will be health to your flesh, and strength to your bones.

PROVERBS 16:24
Pleasant words *are like* a honeycomb, sweetness to the soul and health to the bones.

ISAIAH 45:14
The LORD upholds all who fall, and raises up all *who are* bowed down.

ISAIAH 58:11
The Lord will guide you continually, and satisfy your soul in drought, and strengthen your

Chapter 9 - Healing Scriptures

bones; you shall be like a watered garden, and like a spring of water, whose waters do not fail.

EZEKIEL 37:6-8
I will put sinews on you and bring flesh upon you, cover you with skin and put breath in you; and you shall live. Then you shall know that I *am* the Lord. So I prophesied as I was commanded; and as I prophesied, there was a noise, and suddenly a rattling; and the bones came together, bone to bone. Indeed, as I looked, the sinews and the flesh came upon them, and the skin covered them over; but *there was* no breath in them.

LUKE 13:11-13
And behold, there was a woman who had a spirit of infirmity eighteen years, and was bent over and could in no way raise *herself* up. But when Jesus saw her, He called *her* to *Him* and said to her, "Woman, you are loosed from your infirmity." And He laid *His* hands on her, and immediately she was made straight, and glorified God.

HEALED, IN JESUS' NAME

Cancer

PSALM 30:2-3 (TLB)
O Lord my God, I pleaded with you, and you gave me my health again. You brought me back from the brink of the grave, from death itself, and here I am alive!

PSALM 90:9-10, 14-16
For all our days have passed away in Your wrath; we finish our years like a sigh. The days of our lives are seventy years; and if by reason of strength they are eighty years, yet their boast is only labor and sorrow; for it is soon cut off, and we fly away. Oh, satisfy us early with Your mercy, that we may rejoice and be glad all our days! Make us glad according to the days in which You have afflicted us, the years in which we have seen evil.

PSALM 118:17
I shall not die, but live, and declare the works of the Lord.

PROVERBS 4:20-22
My son, give attention to my words; incline your ear to my sayings. Do not let them depart from

your eyes; keep them in the midst of your heart; for they are life to those who find them, and health to all their flesh.

2 TIMOTHY 1:7
For God has not given us a spirit of fear, but of power and of love and of a sound mind.

2 THESSALONIANS 3:3
But the Lord is faithful, who will establish you and guard you from the evil one.

MATTHEW 15:13
But He answered and said, "Every plant which My heavenly Father has not planted will be uprooted.

Delayed Labour

EXODUS 1:19
And the midwives said to Pharaoh, "Because the Hebrew women are not like the Egyptian women; for they are lively and give birth before the midwives come to them."

HEALED, IN JESUS' NAME

ISAIAH 66:7-9
Before she was in labor, she gave birth; before her pain came, she delivered a male child. Who has heard such a thing? Who has seen such things? Shall the earth be made to give birth in one day? Or shall a nation be born at once? For as soon as Zion was in labor, she gave birth to her children. Shall I bring to the time of birth, and not cause delivery?" says the Lord. "Shall I who cause delivery shut up the womb?" says your God.

Depression, Lack of Sleep, Fear, Unrest or Worry

PSALM 3:5
Trust in the Lord with all your heart, and lean not on your own understanding.

PSALM 4:8
I will both lie down in peace, and sleep; for You alone, O Lord, make me dwell in safety.

PSALM 25:18
Look on my affliction and my pain, and forgive all my sins.

Chapter 9 - Healing Scriptures

PROVERBS 3:21-24

My son, let them (knowledge, understanding, wisdom) not depart from your eyes — keep sound wisdom and discretion; so they will be life to your soul and grace to your neck. Then you will walk safely in your way, and your foot will not stumble. When you lie down, you will not be afraid; yes, you will lie down and your sleep will be sweet.

PROVERBS 12:25

Anxiety in the heart of man causes depression, but a good word makes it glad.

ISAIAH 26:3

You will keep him in perfect peace, whose mind is stayed on You, because he trusts in You.

NAHUM 1:9

What do you conspire against the LORD? He will make an utter end of it. Affliction will not rise up a second time.

HEALED, IN JESUS' NAME

Dumbness and Tongue Impediments

ISAIAH 32:4
Also the heart of the rash will understand knowledge, and the tongue of the stammerers will be ready to speak plainly.

ISAIAH 35:6
Then the lame shall leap like a deer, and the tongue of the dumb sing. for waters shall burst forth in the wilderness, and streams in the desert.

ISAIAH 50:4
"The Lord GOD has given me the tongue of the learned, that I should know how to speak a word in season to *him who is* weary. He awakens me morning by morning, He awakens my ear to hear as the learned.

Eyes and Ears

DEUTERONOMY 34:7
Moses *was* one hundred and twenty years old when he died. His eyes were not dim nor his natural vigour diminished.

Chapter 9 - Healing Scriptures

JOB 36:15
He delivers the poor in their affliction, and opens their ears in oppression.

PSALM 91:3
Surely He shall deliver you from the snare of the fowler and from the perilous pestilence.

PSALM 146:8
The Lord opens the eyes of the blind; the Lord raises those who are bowed down; the Lord loves the righteous.

PROVERBS 20:12 (GNB)
The Lord has given us eyes to see with and ears to listen with.

ISAIAH 29:18
In that day the deaf shall hear the words of the book, and the eyes of the blind shall see out of obscurity and out of darkness.

ISAIAH 32:3
The eyes of those who see will not be dim, and the ears of those who hear will listen.

HEALED, IN JESUS' NAME

ISAIAH 35:5
Then the eyes of the blind shall be opened, and the ears of the deaf shall be unstopped.

ISAIAH 42:18 (GNB)
The LORD says, "Listen, you deaf people! Look closely, you that are blind!"

ISAIAH 50:4-5 (GNB)
The Sovereign LORD has taught me what to say, so that I can strengthen the weary. Every morning he makes me eager to hear what he is going to teach me. The LORD has given me understanding, and I have not rebelled or turned away from him.

MATTHEW 13:16
But blessed *are* your eyes for they see, and your ears for they hear.

HEBREWS 13:8
Jesus Christ is the same yesterday, today, and forever.

As blind Bartimeaus (Mark 10:46-52) received his sight, I shall receive my sight.

Chapter 9 - Healing Scriptures

Facial Outlook, eating disorder, body dystrophic disorder and OCD

PSALM 42:5 and 11

Why are you cast down, O my soul? And why are you disquieted within me? Hope in God, for I shall yet praise Him for the help of His countenance.

Fever

MATTHEW 8:14-17

Now when Jesus had come into Peter's house, He saw his wife's mother lying sick with a fever. So He touched her hand, and the fever left her. And she arose and served them. When evening had come, they brought to Him many who were demon-possessed. And He cast out the spirits with a word, and healed all who were sick, that it might be fulfilled which was spoken by Isaiah the prophet, saying: "He Himself took our infirmities and bore our sicknesses."

LUKE 4:38-39

Now He arose from the synagogue and entered Simon's house. But Simon's wife's mother was sick with a high fever, and they made request of Him concerning her. So He stood over her and rebuked the fever, and it left her. And immediately she arose and served them.

Hair and Hair Loss

MATTHEW 10:29-31
Are not two sparrows sold for a copper coin? And not one of them falls to the ground apart from your Father's will. But the very hairs of your head are all numbered. Do not fear therefore; you are of more value than many sparrows.

ACTS 27:34
Therefore I urge you to take nourishment, for this is for your survival, since not a hair will fall from the head of any of you."

ISAIAH 46:4
Even to *your* old age, I *am* He, and *even* to grey hairs I will carry *you!* I have made, and I will bear; even I will carry, and will deliver *you*.

Chapter 9 - Healing Scriptures

Headaches, Migraines

PSALM 25:18, 20
Look on my affliction and my pain, and forgive all my sins. Keep my soul, and deliver me; let me not be ashamed, for I put my trust in You.

PSALM 119:25, 50
My soul clings to the dust; revive me according to Your word. This is my comfort in my affliction, for Your word has given me life.

JOHN 14:27
Peace I leave with you, My peace I give to you; not as the world gives do I give to you. Let not your heart be troubled, neither let it be afraid.

Heart Diseases

PSALM 27:14
Wait on the Lord; be of good courage, and He shall strengthen your heart; wait, I say, on the Lord!

HEALED, IN JESUS' NAME

PSALM 28:7
The Lord is my strength and my shield; my heart trusted in Him, and I am helped; therefore my heart greatly rejoices, and with my song I will praise Him.

PSALM 31:24
Be of good courage, and He shall strengthen your heart, all you who hope in the Lord.

PSALM 73:26
My flesh and my heart fail; but God is the strength of my heart and my portion forever.

PROVERBS 17:22
A merry heart does good, like medicine, but a broken spirit dries the bones.

Hip Problems

SONG OF SOLOMON 5:15
His legs *are* pillars of marble set on bases of fine gold. His countenance *is* like Lebanon, excellent as the cedars.

Chapter 9 - Healing Scriptures

SONG OF SOLOMON 7:1
How beautiful are your feet in sandals, O prince's daughter! The curves of your thighs *are* like jewels, the work of the hands of a skillful workman.

Kidney Problem

PSALM 119:107
I am afflicted very much; revive me, O LORD, according to Your word.

ISAIAH 53:5
But He was wounded for our transgressions, He was bruised for our iniquities; the chastisement for our peace was upon Him, and by His stripes we are healed.

JEREMIAH 17:14
Heal me, O LORD, and I shall be healed; save me, and I shall be saved, for You are my praise.

HEALED, IN JESUS' NAME

Leg and Feet Problems

1 SAMUEL 2:9
He will guard the feet of His saints, but the wicked shall be silent in darkness. For by strength no man shall prevail.

PROVERBS 3:26
For the LORD will be your confidence, and will keep your foot from being caught.

SONG OF SOLOMON 5:15
His legs *are* pillars of marble set on bases of fine gold. His countenance *is* like Lebanon, Excellent as the cedars.

SONG OF SOLOMON 7:1
How beautiful are your feet in sandals, O prince's daughter! The curves of your thighs *are* like jewels, the work of the hands of a skillful workman.

ISAIAH 35:6
Then the lame shall leap like a deer, and the tongue of the dumb sing. For waters shall burst forth in the wilderness, and streams in the desert.

Chapter 9 - Healing Scriptures

HABAKKUK 3:19
The LORD God is my strength; He will make my feet like deer's *feet*, and He will make me walk on my high hills.

ZECHARIAH 10:12
"So I will strengthen them in the LORD, and they shall walk up and down in His name," says the LORD.

ACTS 3:7
And he took him by the right hand and lifted *him* up, and immediately his feet and ankle bones received strength.

HEBREWS 12:13
And make straight paths for your feet, so that what is lame may not be dislocated, but rather be healed.

Mental Problems

PSALM 25:20
Keep my soul, and deliver me; Let me not be ashamed, for I put my trust in You.

HEALED, IN JESUS' NAME

PSALM 9:9
The LORD also will be a refuge for the oppressed, a refuge in times of trouble.

PROVERBS 12:25
Anxiety in the heart of man causes depression, but a good word makes it glad.

2 TIMOTHY 1:7
For God has not given us a spirit of fear, but of power and of love and of a sound mind.

1 CORINTHIANS 2:16
For "who has known the mind of the LORD that he may instruct Him?" But we have the mind of Christ.

PHILIPPIANS 4:6-7
Be anxious for nothing, but in everything by prayer and supplication, with thanksgiving, let your requests be made known to God; and the peace of God, which surpasses all understanding, will guard your hearts and minds through Christ Jesus.

Chapter 9 - Healing Scriptures

Neck Pain

SONG OF SOLOMON 4:4
Your neck *is* like the tower of David, built for an armoury, on which hang a thousand bucklers, all shields of mighty men.

SONG OF SOLOMON 7:4
Your neck *is* like an ivory tower, your eyes *like* the pools in Heshbon by the gate of Bath Rabbim. Your nose *is* like the tower of Lebanon which looks toward Damascus.

Nervous Conditions

PSALM 46:1
God is our refuge and strength, a very present help in trouble.

PSALM 55:22
Cast your burden on the LORD, and He shall sustain you; He shall never permit the righteous to be moved.

PSALM 147:3
He heals the broken-hearted and binds up their wounds.

HEALED, IN JESUS' NAME

PROVERBS 3:25-26
Do not be afraid of sudden terror, nor of trouble from the wicked when it comes; for the LORD will be your confidence, and will keep your foot from being caught.

2 CORINTHIANS 3:17
Now the Lord is the Spirit; and where the Spirit of the Lord is, there is liberty.

2 THESSALONIANS 3:3
But the Lord is faithful, who will establish you and guard you from the evil one.

Nose Bleed (Epitaxis)

SONG OF SOLOMON 7:4
Your neck *is* like an ivory tower, your eyes *like* the pools in Heshbon by the gate of Bath Rabbim. Your nose *is* like the tower of Lebanon which looks toward Damascus.

Chapter 9 - Healing Scriptures

Palsy, Stokes, Muscular Pains, Sclerosis

PSALM 116:8-10 and PSALM 138:7
For You have delivered my soul from death, my eyes from tears, and my feet from falling. I will walk before the LORD in the land of the living. I believed, therefore I spoke, "I am greatly afflicted." Though I walk in the midst of trouble, You will revive me; You will stretch out Your hand against the wrath of my enemies, and Your right hand will save me.

PROVERBS 3:23
Then you will walk safely in your way, and your foot will not stumble.

Food Poisons

MARK 16:18
They will take up serpents; and if they drink anything deadly, it will by no means hurt them; they will lay hands on the sick, and they will recover."

HEALED, IN JESUS' NAME

Skin Disease

JOB 10:11-12
Clothe me with skin and flesh, and knit me together with bones and sinews? You have granted me life and favour, and Your care has preserved my spirit.

JOB 33:25
His flesh shall be young like a child's, he shall return to the days of his youth.

PROVERBS 3:7-8
Do not be wise in your own eyes; fear the LORD and depart from evil. It will be health to your flesh, and strength to your bones.

PROVERBS 4:20-22
My son, give attention to my words; incline your ear to my sayings. Do not let them depart from your eyes; keep them in the midst of your heart; for they *are* life to those who find them, and health to all their flesh.

EZEKIEL 37:6-8
I will put sinews on you and bring flesh upon you, cover you with skin and put breath in you;

Chapter 9 - Healing Scriptures

and you shall live. Then you shall know that I *am* the LORD. So I prophesied as I was commanded; and as I prophesied, there was a noise, and suddenly a rattling; and the bones came together, bone to bone. Indeed, as I looked, the sinews and the flesh came upon them, and the skin covered them over; but *there was* no breath in them.

DANIEL 1:15
And at the end of ten days their features appeared better and fatter in flesh than all the young men who ate the portion of the king's delicacies.

ROMANS 8:11
But if the Spirit of Him who raised Jesus from the dead dwells in you, He who raised Christ from the dead will also give life to your mortal bodies through His Spirit who dwells in you.

2 CORINTHIANS 4:11
For we who live are always delivered to death for Jesus' sake, that the life of Jesus also may be manifested in our mortal flesh.

HEALED, IN JESUS' NAME

Incurable or Terminal Diseases and Sickness

PSALM 41:3
The LORD will strengthen him on his bed of illness; You will sustain him on his sickbed.

PSALM 42:11
Why are you cast down, O my soul? And why are you disquieted within me? Hope in God; for I shall yet praise Him, The help of my countenance and my God.

Tiredness, Infirmities within body, Weaknesses

PSALM 92:14
They shall still bear fruit in old age; they shall be fresh and flourishing.

ISAIAH 40:29
He gives power to the weak, And to those who have no might He increases strength.

ISAIAH 40:31
But those who wait on the LORD Shall renew their strength; they shall mount up with wings

Chapter 9 - Healing Scriptures

like eagles, they shall run and not be weary, they shall walk and not faint.

ISAIAH 41:10
Fear not, for I am with you; be not dismayed, for I am your God. I will strengthen you, Yes, I will help you, I will uphold you with My righteous right hand.'

ZECHARIAH 10:12
"So I will strengthen them in the LORD, and they shall walk up and down in His name," says the LORD.

Tumour

MATTHEW 15:13
But He answered and said, "Every plant which my heavenly Father has not planted will be uprooted.

Ulcer or Internal Wounds

PSALM 147:3
He heals the broken-hearted and binds up their wounds.

JEREMIAH 30:17

For I will restore health to you and heal you of your wounds,' says the LORD, 'because they called you an outcast saying: "This is Zion; No one seeks her." '

God heals All Diseases

EXODUS 23:25

So you shall serve the LORD your God, and He will bless your bread and your water. And I will take sickness away from the midst of you.

PSALM 34:19

Many are the afflictions of the righteous, but the LORD delivers him out of them all.

PSALM 91:16

With long life I will satisfy him, and show him My salvation."

PSALM 103:1-5

Bless the LORD, O my soul; And all that is within me, bless His holy name! Bless the LORD, O my soul, And forget not all His benefits: Who forgives all your iniquities, Who heals all your diseases, Who redeems your life from destruction, Who crowns you with lovingkindness and tender mercies, Who satisfies your mouth with good things, So that your youth is renewed like the eagle's.

PSALM 107:19-21

Then they cried out to the LORD in their trouble, And He saved them out of their distresses. He sent His word and healed them, and delivered them from their destructions. Oh, that men would give thanks to the LORD for His goodness, And for His wonderful works to the children of men!

PSALM 118:17

I shall not die, but live, and declare the works of the LORD.

JEREMIAH 17:14

Heal me, O LORD, and I shall be healed; Save me, and I shall be saved, for You are my praise.

JEREMIAH 33:6

Behold, I will bring it health and healing; I will heal them and reveal to them the abundance of peace and truth.

HEALED, IN JESUS' NAME

MATTHEW 4:23-24

And Jesus went about all Galilee, teaching in their synagogues, preaching the gospel of the kingdom, and healing all kinds of sickness and all kinds of disease among the people. Then His fame went throughout all Syria; and they brought to Him all sick people who were afflicted with various diseases and torments, and those who were demon-possessed, epileptics, and paralytics; and He healed them.

MATTHEW 8:16-17

When evening had come, they brought to Him many who were demon-possessed. And He cast out the spirits with a word, and healed all who were sick, that it might be fulfilled which was spoken by Isaiah the prophet, saying: "He Himself took our infirmities and bore our sicknesses.

1 PETER 3:12

For the eyes of the LORD are on the righteous, and His ears are open to their prayers; but the face of the LORD is against those who do evil."

JAMES 5:16

Confess your trespasses to one another, and pray for one another, that you may be healed. The

Chapter 9 - Healing Scriptures

effective, fervent prayer of a righteous man avails much.

HEALED, IN JESUS' NAME

CHAPTER 10

"This Belongs to Me"

Several years ago, I religiously listened to Premier Radio, the London flagship Christian radio station. A weekly feature on the station was a healing show with Rev. Major Sam Larbie (Rtd). He made healing so simple, and so unbelievable. Time and again, he would make a simple statement and end with 'Amen', and that was it. The following week, callers would ring in claiming they were healed from previous week's show. I used to say to myself, 'Wait a minute, he really did not pray, so what is the secret?'

I then read his book titled 'Healing is Easy.' The book lay to rest any arguments about healing being the believer's right. He shared countless encounters and the demonstration of the healing power of God in everyday scenarios. His 'secret' lied on the revelation of the word of God he held on to. Leaning on scripture, Bishop Larbie taught that healing is easy because it was already accomplished by the finished work of the cross.

When I decided to write this book, it was easy for me to determine who was to write its foreword; it had to be Bishop Sam Larbie or no one. I believe in the simplicity of the gospel, the finished work of the cross and the power of God. So I tracked him down, and he obliged not only to write the foreword to this book but also gave permission to use his simple statement in the book and my healing ministry. To draw the full benefit of the statement, I would encourage you to pick up the book from any shelf you can find one. Bishop Larbie still uses this statement today in his healing ministry. Following is the extract from his book (used with permission of the Author) starting with the simple statement that has brought healing to thousands.

"This belongs to me, because of what Jesus has done. I received my healing now in Jesus' name. Amen."

Chapter 10 - "This Belongs To Me"

It is a known fact that Jesus did not use a formula when he healed people. He employed different methods in different situations. The Lord himself said that he did what he saw his father doing.

The 'This belongs to me' prayer may be seen as a formula but it is not. It is not a magical incantation that results in healing. It is a condensed form of Isaiah 53:4-5.

Surely He has borne our griefs and carried our sorrows; yet we esteemed Him stricken, smitten by God, and afflicted. But He was wounded for our transgressions, He was bruised for our iniquities; the chastisement for our peace was upon Him, and by His stripes we are healed.

The emphasis is on what Jesus has done so that we can receive healing from him. Whoever prays for healing should have no shadow of doubt in his mind that the work done at Calvary is complete. The promise is a sure one! No wonder verse four of Isaiah 53 begins with the word surely. It is a certainty, a confirmation and an indisputable assurance. God has covenanted to continue to heal all who are sick and weak to fulfil the words he spoke through is servant Isaiah.

HEALED, IN JESUS' NAME

He was a voluntary bearer

Surely He has borne our griefs and carried our sorrows.

The burdens were transferred to a voluntary bearer who willingly took on board the sin of all humanity. He accepted that awesome responsibility. Friend, this is Jesus for you!

The Son of God declared on the cross at Calvary, "It is finished." The purpose for which he had come had been accomplished. It was a job well done, and nothing could be taken away from it.

He did not hold the Roman guards responsible; neither did he blame the Jewish authorities. It was His Father's sovereign plan to use this means to reconcile man to Himself.

We serve a living Saviour, Who used no set method to heal. He sometimes spoke the word of healing. Sometimes the sick touched Him. But whatever He did, He was inspired by His Father to do. And in our time too we should remember that Jesus Christ is the same yesterday, today and forever!

Believe that as you say these prayers in faith, the Lord will heal you now. It is already done.

Chapter 10 - "This Belongs To Me"

Your portion is just to receive from the Lord. It is no formula! For Emphasis, let me say it again.

"This belongs to me, because of what Jesus has done. I received my healing now in Jesus' name. Amen."

HEALED, IN JESUS' NAME

CHAPTER 11

It Makes Sense

I promised at the beginning of the book to address some of the issues raised after I posted my testimony online. Following are my responses to the concerns.

Heaven and Hell

I mentioned at the beginning that it felt as if I was in hell. For clarity, let me repeat the statement.

'Just like that, I was ablaze. I lost any sense of my surrounding. "Where am I? Am I alive or am

I dead? In hell or earth, where am I?" Those were the questions that ran through my mind.[1]

Why was I thinking like that, you may ask?

First, I do not believe there will be a fire or burning in heaven. This is what the Bible teaches. If I was burning, I must be in hell or hell must have come to earth.

Secondly, I do not believe I would not make heaven and end up in hell. I made that decision 31 years before the incident. I've been translated from the Kingdom of darkness to the kingdom of His dear Son, Jesus. Again, this is what my Bible taught me.

Heaven is real; hell is real. If truly I were in hell, I must have gone there for a different reason. Maybe so I can understand the torments awaiting the children of disobedience. Since my ordeal, I have a greater sympathy for lost souls, and I believe I now feel the heart of God for the unsaved.

Emergency calls

Why did I not think to call the emergency services as plan A, but instead as plan B?

Chapter 11 - It Makes Sense

I have tried to explain this earlier but would like to add to it. I chose what at the time appeared best. I was not in the perfect frame of mind. With the benefit of hindsight, I would advise anyone in my position to call the emergency service first, no matter how good your spouse is. These are my reasons:

You save time and save yourself. If you called your spouse and though they can diagnose or assess your condition, they may not have the right facilities, tools, or equipment to deal with the situation. If you then decide to call the emergency service after, you would have lost time. For minor injuries or incidents, please avoid calling the already overworked service so they can attend to more severe needs.

Secondly, the emergency operators will connect you to a virtual help while you wait for the right services to arrive. The virtual services are trained to monitor your condition and to keep you alive before the specialists arrive.

Thirdly, the emergency operators can dispatch the right services based on your need. You spouse may be a good doctor, but they may not be able to put fire out of a burning building.

HEALED, IN JESUS' NAME

The Medical Service and Medicine

Some people are not sure about the role of medicine and medical professionals when it comes to the subject of healing.

First, let me make my position very clear; doctors can treat, but only God heals. The doctors cannot cure whom God has decided He would not heal. The power to heal is in His hands. Money can buy medicine, but it cannot buy health or healing.

However, God has provided the knowledge and skill to tackle particular problems. Any knowledge that He reveals or hides proves He is still in charge. We only get ourselves on the wrong side when we take the knowledge and refuse to acknowledge its source or use it for our selfish motives.

When I had the burn, the first person I called was the healer 'Jesus'. I did not have to pray a long prayer in the fire. I just called the name 'Jesus'. You need to put God first in any and every difficult circumstance. Many people put God as the last resort. Examples are: the disciples sinking on the sea; the woman with the issue of blood; Apostle Peter fishing; and many more. No, God should come first.

Chapter 11 - It Makes Sense

After that, I called my wife, first as my wife, but also as a medical professional. Would I have taken her medical advice or treatment? YES, I would. Then I called the emergency services and followed every bit of advice, treatment and medications prescribed, while I continued praying. Please tell me what is wrong with that?

I read a book that was written by Dodie Osteen of Lakewood Church, John Osteen's wife and Joel Osteen's mum. She was diagnosed with metastatic adenocarcinoma [cancer] of the liver in 1981. She, however, refused doctor's treatment as she stood on the finished work of Calvary. She only trusted God and prayed for her healing. She continued to claim and declare God's promises on divine health and divine healing. She was completely healed.

In the same book, I also read that she had a hysterectomy. She battled whether to have the surgery or not, but finally consented. Examination under anaesthesia immediately before surgery revealed the golf ball-sized mass on the wall of her uterus. After surgery, when the pathologist ran the necessary tests for his report, no tumour could be found. It was a miracle![1]

My point is that, at one point, Dodie refused treatment based on her conviction and at another instance; she received help from medical science.

[1]. Osteen D. (1986). Healed of Cancer. Houston, Texas.

Saved by the prayers of the saints

The prayer of agreement produces greater power. I want to appreciate members of our Church for standing by me during my ordeal especially in the place of prayer.

If you are going through a difficult patch, you need to surround yourself with people who can hold you up in prayer. However, not everyone is qualified to be informed of your issues; inform only those who matter. The only people that were told of the burn were my church members. Even my extended family in and outside the UK did not know until months later, when the testimony was shared.

This is my point; there are people who cannot help you but rather make matters more complicated for you. Remember the story of the Shunammite woman whose only son died. She did not inform her husband and Gehazi, Elisha's servant, that the boy was dead. She told them both that everything was well. She knew they could not do anything about the situation. Whereas, when she met with Elisha, she poured out her bitter anguish to him. He was in a position to help. He was instrumental in the boy's birth.

Don't organise a pity-party or involve those that are negative and discouraging whereas you need faith, and hope.

The angel of death

I told, in the main story, that I saw an angel of death. How was I so sure? Well, to the best of my understanding, it looked like one. I knew that the fire was meant to kill me, and a strange creature accompanied it.

Angels are integral part of our existence and survival on earth. They are there at birth, in life and death. They can be chosen instruments unto good or evil assignments depending on who the master is. The devil is declared, in the Bible, as possessing the power of death, and he uses his angels to accomplish his purpose.

The following scriptures summarises the roles of angels.

HEALED, IN JESUS' NAME

MATTHEW 18:10
Take heed that you do not despise one of these little ones, for I say to you that in heaven their angels always see the face of My Father who is in heaven.

HEBREWS 1:13-14
But to which of the angels has He ever said: "Sit at My right hand, till I make Your enemies Your footstool"? Are they not all ministering spirits sent forth to minister for those who will inherit salvation?

PSALMS 91:11
For He shall give His angels charge over you, to keep you in all your ways.

PSALMS 34:7
The angel of the LORD encamps all around those who fear Him, and delivers them.

MARK 1:13
And He was there in the wilderness forty days, tempted by Satan, and was with the wild beasts; and the angels ministered to Him.

Chapter 11 - It Makes Sense

MATTHEW 4:11
Then the devil left Him, and behold, angels came and ministered to Him.

LUKE 16:22
So it was that the beggar died, and was carried by the angels to Abraham's bosom. The rich man also died and was buried.

HEBREWS 2:14
Inasmuch then as the children have partaken of flesh and blood, He Himself likewise shared in the same, that through death He might destroy him who had the power of death, that is, the devil,

The dreams and warnings

God wants to reveal things to us before they happen. It is a shame that most of us are not sensitive to His voice or nudging. He would like for us to know both of His intentions and activities and those of the devil. I knew by revelation that there was something on the way. At first, I prayed, on the understanding and by my experience, that God always answer my prayers. After the second revelation, I got the church involved because of its content. When I had experiences similar to this one in the past, I had personally broken through. However, I had also seen the devil attack my other interests, especially my extended family; something similar to Job's ordeal.

Unfortunately, on Monday of the same week we prayed at church, members' extended families were attacked.

AMOS 3:7
Surely the Lord GOD does nothing, unless He reveals His secret to His servants the prophets.

GENESIS 18:17-18
And the LORD said, "Shall I hide from Abraham what I am doing, since Abraham shall surely become a great and mighty nation, and all the nations of the earth shall be blessed in him?

Then I had a third dream. This time, I knew the battle was still on. Before I could build a prayer network, I was struck. The devil's intention was to strike the shepherd so the sheep would scatter. Surprisingly, the devil's attack made the church stronger.

I tasted death. I only had twenty percent burn. It was the devil's attack. God had revealed the

Chapter 11 - It Makes Sense

devil's intention, allowed me to experience the burn, through the prayer of the saints, made sure it was light, and calling on the name of 'Jesus', healed me afterwards.

As I said in the main story, two things lessened the experience: taking my top off and moving the barbecue set to the middle of the garden.

Why was I a target?

If you serve God wholeheartedly, the devil will be very unhappy. The devil is upset with every child of God walking in the light and serving God. He usually does not bother those that compromise and are unserious about their relationship with God. He already has their loyalty, so why should he attack his own?

Secondly, the more threatening you are to the kingdom of darkness, the more ferocious are the attacks from the devil.

I was at the time of the attack putting together a national programme for our denomination, for which we had had many prayers and planning. Just three weeks to the event, I was attacked. He wanted to kill me so the event would have either been affected or cancelled.

Also, praising God disturbs and weakens the enemy. I hope you know that Lucifer was the archangel in charge of worship in heaven before he was thrown down to earth. Moreover, since his position has been occupied by 'praisers', he has been unhappy. That is why the most attacked team or church department is the praise and worship team.

We were entering the third week of our praise month when the devil attacked. In September, we spend the entire worship services praising God. Added to this, it was just days before my next birthday which happened to fall on a Sunday. I immediately understood why I was attacked; our praise programme was effective.

If you praised God and are attacked, praise Him more. If you served God and are attacked, serve Him more. It simply means you are doing something right. It means you are being recognised in heaven. It only means your ministering is working. Shame the devil, make him madder. It is not the time to be scared or sorry for yourself.

I went to every service until I became completely healed. My face was messed up, but my faith was dressed up. My face was damaged, but my feet were strengthened. I became more active. I carried on organising the convention. I

Chapter 11 - It Makes Sense

even convened the programmes. I became unstoppable. That is the way to defeat the enemy. Had I given in, the devil would just have succeeded. Though I could not be physically killed, I would have been spiritually derailed. I understood what Apostle Paul went through, and I showed it was possible to remain standing.

2 CORINTHIANS 6:1-10

We then, as workers together with Him also plead with you not to receive the grace of God in vain. For He says: "In an acceptable time I have heard you, and in the day of salvation I have helped you." Behold, now is the accepted time; behold, now is the day of salvation. We give no offence in anything, that our ministry may not be blamed. But in all things we commend ourselves as ministers of God: in much patience, in tribulations, in needs, in distresses, in stripes, in imprisonments, in tumults, in labours, in sleeplessness, in fastings; by purity, by knowledge, by long-suffering, by kindness, by the Holy Spirit, by sincere love, by the word of truth, by the power of God, by the armour of righteousness on the right hand and on the left, by honour and dishonour, by evil report and good report; as deceivers, and yet true; as unknown, and yet well known; as dying, and behold we live; as chastened, and yet not killed;

as sorrowful, yet always rejoicing; as poor, yet making many rich; as having nothing, and yet possessing all things.